Towards Jerusalem

The Bible Reading Fellowship
15 The Chambers, Vineyard
Abingdon OX14 3FE
brf.org.uk

The Bible Reading Fellowship (BRF) is a Registered Charity (233280)

ISBN 978 0 85746 560 3
First published 2017
10 9 8 7 6 5 4 3 2 1 0
All rights reserved

Acknowledgements
Unless otherwise stated, scripture quotations are taken from The Holy Bible, New
International Version (Anglicised edition) copyright © 1979, 1984, 2011 by Biblica.
Used by permission of Hodder & Stoughton Publishers, an Hachette UK company.
All rights reserved. 'NIV' is a registered trademark of Biblica. UK trademark number
1448790.

Scripture quotations from The Revised Standard Version of the Bible, copyright ©
1946, 1952, 1971 by the Division of Christian Education of the National Council of
the Churches of Christ in the United States of America. Used by permission. All rights
reserved.

Extracts from the Authorised Version of the Bible (The King James Bible), the rights
in which are vested in the Crown, are reproduced by permission of the Crown's
Patentee, Cambridge University Press.

Scripture quotations taken from the New English Bible, copyright © Cambridge
University Press and Oxford University Press 1961, 1970. All rights reserved.

Every effort has been made to trace and contact copyright owners for material used
in this resource. We apologise for any inadvertent omissions or errors, and would
ask those concerned to contact us so that full acknowledgement can be made in the
future.

A catalogue record for this book is available from the British Library

Printed and bound by CPI Group (UK) Ltd, Croydon CR0 4YY

Steve Brady

Towards Jerusalem

A pilgrim's regress and progress
to God's Holy City

Dedicated to the memory of my parents, 'Our Jim' (1918–2003), an ex-PoW and Liverpool bus driver, and 'Big Ede' (1923–2017), a woman of immense vitality and industry, who sadly departed this life as this book was nearing completion. Two remarkable people, married for over 50 years, who were generous to a fault, and enriched many – especially their family – by their unconditional love.

Contents

Introduction

I love the countryside. But by birth and temperament I'm a city dweller. This last century particularly has witnessed the astonishing growth of cities, in particular huge metropolises of millions of people, squeezed into ghettoes, housing estates and high-rise apartments. One city, however, has a unique profile. From ancient times, Jerusalem, or Zion, has not only been a location on a map of the Middle East, but a well-worn metaphor for human aspiration and desire, of conflict and pain. Who is unaware that the present city of Jerusalem is the very centre of controversy for Jew and Arab, Israeli and Palestinian? Christian hymns may still fulminate about 'Jerusalem the golden' and 'Glorious things of thee are spoken, Zion city of our God', but the fact is that Jerusalem is to many people a synonym for pain, division and injustice – a veritable political and religious hot potato.

Whatever huge differences and difficulties exist between Jews, Christians and Muslims, all three share a common belief that Jerusalem, literally and metaphorically, is anything but a footnote on the page of world events; it is most definitely part of the main text of human history and destiny. Indeed, Jerusalem has a long and chequered history, both instructive and fascinating. But that cannot detain us here. For the intention of these meditations is not to address all the attendant questions that arise when Jerusalem is mentioned, but far more modestly to ask what has Jerusalem, and the metaphors and similes it suggests, alongside other cities we'll mention these next few weeks, to do with the life of faith and the Lenten road to Easter.

Towards Jerusalem is the title of a book of devotional poems by Amy Carmichael, which I first encountered over 40 years ago.[1] Her insights into the spiritual life are so often profound and challenging, and have called me to *progress* when I was thinking of *regress*, hence the subtitle of this book, *A pilgrim's regress and progress to God's Holy City*. Paul McCartney, of the Beatles, sang about 'the long and winding road'. The journey on the road that leads to the city of God, as I hope we will discover as we walk with the Master these weeks, may also be experienced as a journey to freedom. How? Because on the pilgrim's way, we may be joined by the one who 'resolutely set out for Jerusalem' to redeem us (Luke 9:51). Jesus now invites us to walk with him, through cross and resurrection, to eternal life in the city of God. May we sense afresh that 'Jesus himself came up and walked along' with us (Luke 24:15).

Ash Wednesday

....

Temptations

Then Jesus was led by the Spirit into the wilderness to be tempted by the devil. After fasting forty days and forty nights, he was hungry. The tempter came to him and said, 'If you are the Son of God, tell these stones to become bread.'

Jesus answered, 'It is written: "Man shall not live on bread alone, but on every word that comes from the mouth of God."'

Then the devil took him to the holy city and had him stand on the highest point of the temple. 'If you are the Son of God,' he said, 'throw yourself down. For it is written:

"He will command his angels concerning you,
and they will lift you up in their hands,
so that you will not strike your foot against a stone."'

Jesus answered him, 'It is also written: "Do not put the Lord your God to the test."'

Again, the devil took him to a very high mountain and showed him all the kingdoms of the world and their splendour. 'All this I will give you,' he said, 'if you will bow down and worship me.'

Jesus said to him, 'Away from me, Satan! For it is written: "Worship the Lord your God, and serve him only."'

Then the devil left him, and angels came and attended him.

MATTHEW 4:1–11

Traditionally, 1 March is a great day for the Welsh, being St David's Day, the day of their patron saint. In 2017, it coincided with Ash

Wednesday, which marks the beginning of Lent and is often overlooked by the media. However, the Scottish MP Carol Monaghan caused a media stir that day at a House of Commons select committee. A practising Catholic, she appeared with a cross etched in ash upon her forehead, a traditional symbol for Ash Wednesday. Although many people didn't know what it meant, one member of the committee asked her about it, as the session was going to be broadcast. 'I think they just thought I didn't want to be embarrassed – but I was not going to rub it off,' she said. It raises the interesting debate of visible religious symbols and devotional practices, whether Christian or other, in the public square, which won't detain us here. Not all Christians observe either Ash Wednesday or Lent. For example, the Eastern Orthodox Church observes Lent, but marks its beginning with Clean Monday. So why Ash Wednesday? Why not start Lent on, for example, a Thursday? The reason is that it is exactly forty days before Easter Sunday, not counting the intervening Sundays. Hence it is always a Wednesday.

More importantly, what is the significance and purpose of Lent? During Lent, the Anglican Church's calendar directs its readers to Christ's temptations, his 40 days of fasting and temptation in the desert. At one level, reading this account, we might conclude that the big lesson is that temptations and trials can come in a variety of ways, but Jesus overcame them and so may we, especially if we fast and pray. There is certainly some truth in that application. Indeed, one of my friends, facing massive problems with his daughter's drug abuse, embarked on a 40-day fast for her salvation and recovery. She is now happily married and walking with God.

But there's more in this narrative, of course. It tells us something about what has been called 'the fair face of evil'. For example, the devil's suggestion of a 'stones into bread' trick would certainly make Jesus a hit with the crowd, as it did in his subsequent ministry when, having fed the 5,000, they sought to make him king, although he deliberately withdrew from them (John 6:15). But if Jesus was diverted into delivering bread for this world, how could he deliver 'the Bread of Life' for the next? The second temptation calls for another display of power, and to become perhaps a celebrated ancient illusionist, equivalent to the likes of Harry Houdini or the more contemporary David Blaine or Dynamo. It's always possible to draw a crowd by tricks, but keeping them for the more serious business of heaven is altogether different. The third temptation is the ultimate celebrity prize; it is what every strongman down the ages has craved – world domination! And how appealing to take the broad road to success and avoid the narrow road of pain, rejection, suffering and death on a cross. It is possible to 'gain the whole world' by illegitimate means and in the process forfeit one's own soul (Mark 8:36). By the way, by what right did the devil offer 'all the kingdoms of the world' (v. 8), when 'The earth is the Lord's… the world, and all who live in it' (Psalm 24:1)?

Like Ash Wednesday, Lent is not mentioned in the Bible, so scripture neither forbids nor enjoins its practice. Accordingly, Christians can prayerfully decide on how or whether to use this 40-day period. For example, Prime Minister Theresa May, a vicar's daughter and practising Christian, confessed that she had given up crisps for Lent in 2017. Others, like MP Carol Monaghan, may decide to have the sign of a cross on their forehead. More importantly, since Lent offers a specific period for self-examination, self-denial and the forsaking of our sinful habits, it is also a reminder that repenting of our sins and identifying with Christ is not only for 40-odd days a year. The Olympic marathon runner and gold medallist at the 1969 European Championships and 1970 Commonwealth Games, Ron Hill, has run at least one mile every day. Between 20 December 1964 and the end of January 2017, when he had to miss a day, he had clocked up, by my estimate, some 19,032 consecutive days of running at least a mile. So, we begin and continue this Lent our journey *Towards Jerusalem*. My prayer is that whatever these next 40-plus days may hold, there will be more *progress* than *regress* that will keep us going every day, long after Lent, as Easter people, denying ourselves, taking up our cross and following the crucified one.

Thursday

....

Blessed are the balanced

Brothers and sisters, if someone is caught in a sin, you who live by the Spirit should restore that person gently. But watch yourselves, or you also may be tempted. Carry each other's burdens, and in this way you will fulfil the law of Christ. If anyone thinks they are something when they are not, they deceive themselves. Each one should test their own actions. Then they can take pride in themselves alone, without comparing themselves to someone else, for each one should carry their own load.

GALATIANS 6:1–5

To be honest, although I was in my 50s and had never tried it, there was a bit of self-confidence. I reckoned that as I still played some football, which requires some equilibrium, then learning to ski would not be too much hassle. Now, imagine a newborn giraffe wearing roller skates trying to dance on ice; that does not come close to how bad I was at doing what is essential to skiing – keeping my balance. The Christian life is always a matter of balance, though there is no verse that says 'Blessed are the balanced!' However, in this passage, such balance is helpfully illustrated by the two phrases 'Carry each other's burdens' and 'each one should carry their own load' (vv. 2, 5).

As I write this, into my mind comes an image of my dad as a younger man, with two huge, heavy suitcases, one in each hand, struggling along a road in Dublin, sweat pouring off him, as we four family members made our way from the overnight ferry to the rail station. His conviction was that the two cases kept him balanced, so the rest of us just cheered him on. But what happens when, metaphorically, we have three, four or more such cases to carry? We have a word for it – overloaded. Like trucks, people have different load capacities. Some seem to be 'forty-tonners', and seemingly capable of pulling a trailer load behind them as well. Others seem to have the mere capacity of the Deliveroo cycles that I increasingly see darting around town delivering pizza.

At one level, we are wise to know our limits. There are occasions when a conglomeration of burdens arrives in our lives that we just cannot personally carry. In attempting simply to carry on regardless, we might do ourselves and others real damage. The chaplain of Moorlands College, Jonathan Woodhouse, was for many years an army chaplain, rising to the dizzy heights of Chaplain-General. We were recently viewing an image from the Afghan war of four British soldiers, one on each corner of the stretcher, carrying to safety a wounded colleague. He reminded me that it is a non-negotiable value of the British Army that when a soldier is down their comrades, risking their own lives if necessary, will be there for them. That is one reason why we need church: not buildings, of course, but fellow believers engaged in the same battles and looking out for each other. 'But pity anyone who falls and has no one to help them up', warns Ecclesiastes (4:10). Lent is a great opportunity to reconnect with church, for we need other believers.

On the other side of the coin is the kind of person who expects everyone else to fetch and carry for them. They seem unwilling to 'carry their own load'. In fact, what appears to be only hand luggage to most people is to them a huge, overweight bag. So, as they contemplate boarding the plane for their journey, they expect their baggage to be transported at someone else's expense. Failing that, they complain until some poor, guilt-ridden baggage handler takes the strain for them, while they sit back and travel first class. Unfortunately, ease and comfort rarely make great people. Selfishness and laziness are not the way of the crucified one, who never thought 'me' but 'thee'! But self-giving love leaves indelible memories. For example, there is a delightful vignette of a giver rather than a taker in the story of Tabitha (or Dorcas in Greek), whom Peter raised from the dead. 'All the widows stood around him, crying and showing him the robes and other clothing that Dorcas had made while she was still with them' (Acts 9:39). The nuance of 'showing him' is probably that they were wearing what she had lovingly made for them. One of my friends had an old workhorse of a car that was called Tabitha. 'Why?' I enquired. 'Because, like her namesake, she's full of good works!'

Lent is an opportunity to discover and recover our spiritual balance. If you are overloaded, find a few friends to share your burden with before the Lord. And if, in all honesty, you're travelling light, then to adapt a phrase from John F. Kennedy's 1961 inauguration address: 'Ask not what others can do for you, ask what you can do for others.'

Friday

··

The ultimate mission statement

When Jesus came to the region of Caesarea Philippi, he asked his disciples, 'Who do people say the Son of Man is?'

They replied, 'Some say John the Baptist; others say Elijah; and still others, Jeremiah or one of the prophets.'

'But what about you?' he asked. 'Who do you say I am?'

Simon Peter answered, 'You are the Messiah, the Son of the living God.'

Jesus replied, 'Blessed are you, Simon son of Jonah, for this was not revealed to you by flesh and blood, but by my Father in heaven. And I tell you that you are Peter, and on this rock I will build my church, and the gates of Hades will not overcome it. I will give you the keys of the kingdom of heaven; whatever you bind on earth will be bound in heaven, and whatever you loose on earth will be loosed in heaven.' Then he ordered his disciples not to tell anyone that he was the Messiah.

From that time on Jesus began to explain to his disciples that he must go to Jerusalem and suffer many things at the hands of the elders, the chief priests and the teachers of the law, and that he must be killed and on the third day be raised to life.

Peter took him aside and began to rebuke him. 'Never, Lord!' he said. 'This shall never happen to you!'

Jesus turned and said to Peter, 'Get behind me, Satan! You are a stumbling block to me; you do not have in mind the concerns of God, but merely human concerns.'

MATTHEW 16:13–23

Mission statements: these days, it seems like every organisation needs one. At best, they are concise statements of purpose that everyone on the team can understand and identify with. So, a hospital's mission statement might be 'to deliver first-class medical care to our patients'. An investment bank might promise 'to provide a high-yield, low-risk return for our customers'. At Moorlands College, we exist 'to equip people, passionate about Jesus Christ, to impact the church and the world'. A friend's church uses just ten words: 'To see lost people become committed followers of Jesus Christ'. Or, as someone quipped, the average church's statement might be: 'Our mission is one day to discover our mission'. In today's reading, following immediately on from Peter's great confession (v. 16) Jesus announces his mission statement: 'I will build my church!' (v. 18).

What great *commitment* that exudes. When Jesus uttered those words in Caesarea Philippi, perhaps in the shadow of the shrine dedicated to the Greek god Pan, the idea of his creating a new community of people, his church, must have appeared ludicrous. Its absurdity would have been heightened by his speaking, a few verses later, of his impending death, which prompted Peter's rebuke. But herein lies the great secret of the church's future growth and development. For the one who in a short while would die on a cross, giving his 'life as a ransom for many' (Matthew 20:28), in the same breath speaks of his resurrection: 'on the third day be(ing) raised to life' (v. 21). Founders of companies, organisations and nations rarely live long enough to see even a small amount of the fruit of their endeavours. But as Jesus commissions his people, in the final verses of Matthew's Gospel, to take his good news everywhere, he promises to be with them always. How? Because he is the risen one, our great and available contemporary Lord.

Christ's *commitment* is tempered by the reality of *conflict*: 'the gates of Hades'. In essence, that phrase represents anything and everything that gets in the way of his coming kingdom – his righteous rule that brings forgiveness, peace with God and hope to a world full of 'sin cities', the repositories of misery, pain, injustice and death.

Sometimes, the opposition comes from outside: Christians are, after all, part of a martyrs' faith. Other times, the opposition comes from within the very church Jesus promises to build. There are churches that simply do not want to change or be Christ's agents of change; forgetting that they are called to be 'a city on a hill' (Matthew 5:14), they deteriorate into becoming candles blown out by the wind. Likewise, individual Christians can peddle their own agendas, forgetting to seek first God's kingdom (Matthew 6:33) and building their own petty fiefdoms instead.

Allied to the reality of Christ's *commitment*, and despite the *conflicts*, his words breathe total *confidence*. The 18th-century philosopher bishop Joseph Butler turned down the archbishopric of Canterbury, because he believed it was 'too late to try to support a falling Church'. That was in 1747! By the end of that century, however, multitudes in Great Britain and America had joined the church of Jesus as waves of revival swept over those nations, names like George Whitfield and John Wesley being indelibly etched in the church's history. In 1848, John Geddie left his pastorate in New London, Prince Edward Island, Canada, and headed for a cannibals' island in the South Pacific. His mission was so successful, and the love of the islanders for him so great, that years later a plaque was unveiled on the wall of his mission church on Aneityum Island. It said:

When he landed in 1848
There were no Christians here.
When he left in 1872
There were no heathen.

In the late 1940s, the church in China was about one million strong when Mao Zedong's revolution commenced, inflicting massive suffering on Christians. Today, that church numbers tens of millions. And all over the world, sometimes with just a handful of people, at other times in their thousands, Christians gather to worship and serve the Lord. How come? Because Jesus said, 'I will build my church.'

Despite the idiosyncrasies, hypocrisies and, at times, the shocking failures of individual Christians and churches, Jesus promises to accomplish his mission. And he calls people like ourselves – in need of his forgiveness, transformation and empowerment – to be part of his mission to his world, echoed in the Lord's Prayer: 'your kingdom come, your will be done, on earth as it is in heaven' (Matthew 6:10). Recall the old Wayside Pulpit challenge: 'Carpenter from Nazareth seeks joiners'. We're still invited to join: 'Come to me,' says Jesus, 'take my yoke upon you' – that is, get involved in the action – 'and you will find rest for your souls' (Matthew 11:28–29). This Lent, the mission director awaits our response.

Runners and spectators

Therefore, since we are surrounded by such a great cloud of witnesses, let us throw off everything that hinders and the sin that so easily entangles. And let us run with perseverance the race marked out for us, fixing our eyes on Jesus, the pioneer and perfecter of faith. For the joy set before him he endured the cross, scorning its shame, and sat down at the right hand of the throne of God. Consider him who endured such opposition from sinners, so that you will not grow weary and lose heart.

HEBREWS 12:1–3

The traditional story is inspirational. So inspiring, in fact, that millions who have never heard his name immediately recognise a kindred spirit when they learn of his feat. Over two days, in 490BC, he ran some 150 miles from Athens to Sparta, asking for help when the Persians landed at Marathon. Subsequently, he ran some 25 miles to announce Athens' victory over Persia, and upon arrival reputedly said, '*Chairete nikomen*' – 'Greetings (or Rejoice!), we are the victors' – then collapsed and died. His name was Pheidippides, or possibly Philippides.

The Christian life is not a sprint, always a marathon, and we are urged to run the race of faith not to Sparta or Athens but to 'the Holy City, the new Jerusalem', that one day will descend like a beautiful bride on her wedding day, eclipsing all our broken, ruined, marred and wicked cities, as God makes 'all things new' (Revelation 21:2, 5). Are you ready to run?

Join the race

Recently, under the auspices of the Japan Keswick Convention, I happened to be staying at the Keio Plaza Hotel in central Tokyo. When I arrived, I did not know that the Tokyo Marathon was due to start from that very spot in a couple of days. Soon, runners of all shapes and sizes, colours and creeds, nations and languages were staying at the hotel. I loved it, having been a bit of a distance runner myself. I drank in the atmosphere, chatted to various competitors and looked something of the part, I thought, in my New Balance trainers and training top. I felt somewhat gratified by the folks who asked, despite my being older, if I would be running. Although over 27,000 people would be, I wouldn't, for I had not applied and been accepted for the race. It can be that way with faith. We may look the part, act the part and hang around with those who run faith's race, enjoying all the bonhomie, yet we have never personally applied to Christ for entrance to his marathon. Have you? The Lord does not call us to be spectators but participants.

Keep up the pace

Some have suggested that the 'great cloud of witnesses' (v. 1), a reference back to the deceased worthies and not-so-worthies of the previous chapter, are somehow spectators of our race on earth. How boring that would be for them. Rather, the gallery of faith, as it has been called, is a bit like my experience a few years ago being shown around Liverpool FC's academy (not an easy assignment for a lifelong Evertonian). On one corridor wall was a line of photos of those who had come through the youth academy and made it into the Premier League, players like Steven Gerrard and Michael Owen. That gallery was there to inspire a new generation of would-be Liverpool greats – they did it, why not you?

Faith's marathon needs to be run 'with perseverance', following not our own course but 'the race marked out for us'. Any distance runner knows that there are things that 'hinder' and 'entangle', and so need to be discarded (v. 1). We need to wear the spiritual equivalent of trainers that give us New Balance, growing like Jesus 'in wisdom and stature, and in favour with God and people' – that is, intellectually, physically, spiritually and relationally (Luke 2:52). And we need shoes branded ASICS – Anima Sana In Corpere Sano ('a sound mind in a sound body') – aiming for such if health and strength and the years permit.

Complete the course

Most people can start a marathon; the trick is to finish it. It is wise, therefore, not to concentrate on how poorly I feel I am doing compared to my fellow-runners, how tough the course is, how short a distance I have travelled, or how bad I am going to feel in recovery tomorrow. One thing needs my concentration: the finishing tape! Somehow, it helps to set my internal body clock and keeps me focused: there will be a finale. So, the 'fixing' referred to here (v. 2) has the nuance of looking away from other distractions, so that we give undivided attention to Jesus. Too many drop out of the race because they look around at what others are or are not doing, or start looking back or within, and fail to 'consider' carefully (v. 3), and focus on the Lord Jesus himself. An old chorus speaks of 'turning our eyes upon Jesus', looking 'full in his wonderful face' and finding everything else growing 'strangely dim in the light of his glory and grace'.

As we enter the marathon of Lent, I want to invite you afresh to run to 'Mount Zion, to the city of the living God, the heavenly Jerusalem' (Hebrews 12:22). Whatever regress the past months may have witnessed, now is the time to 'kit up and crack on', as one of my friends regularly reminds me to do. And you may discover your shoes become a pair of Nike – the Greek for victory. Get running!

Week 1

....

Seeking a city: unfamiliar people and places

John Lennox, the Christian apologist and professor of mathematics at the University of Oxford, opens his book *Seven Days that Divide the World* by reminiscing how profoundly the opening words of Genesis, 'In the beginning, God created the heavens and the earth', affected him on Christmas Eve 1968. The crew of Apollo 8 had broadcast the words as they orbited the moon. Here, at one of the heights of human achievement in science and technology, 'The biblical announcement of the fact of creation was as timelessly clear as it was magnificently appropriate.'[2] Another friend, Alasdair Paine, a vicar in Cambridge, has written a helpful little book appropriately titled *The First Chapters of Everything*, along with the explanatory subtitle *How Genesis 1–4 explains our world*.[3] Both books are a rewarding read.

It is not my intention in this first full week of Lent to meander through the early chapters of Genesis. I did so in a previous BRF book, *The Incredible Journey*.[4] Rather, I hope we may drop in on a number of characters and their location en route through Genesis. Such characters may be viewed as the good, the bad and the ugly – to quote the 1966 Spaghetti Western – for here we find both regress and progress in the lives of wandering people, pilgrims indeed, who are searching for a home, God's Holy City. We join them in their quest.

....

From a garden to a city

After he drove the man out, he placed on the east side of the Garden of Eden cherubim and a flaming sword flashing back and forth to guard the way to the tree of life.

'You will be a restless wanderer on the earth.'

Cain said to the Lord, 'My punishment is more than I can bear. Today you are driving me from the land, and I will be hidden from your presence; I will be a restless wanderer on the earth, and whoever finds me will kill me.'

But the Lord said to him, 'Not so; anyone who kills Cain will suffer vengeance seven times over.' Then the Lord put a mark on Cain so that no one who found him would kill him. So Cain went out from the Lord's presence and lived in the land of Nod, east of Eden.

Cain made love to his wife, and she became pregnant and gave birth to Enoch. Cain was then building a city, and he named it after his son Enoch.

GENESIS 3:24; 4:12B–17

Mention the garden of Eden in polite company, and folk may smile condescendingly at you. Mention it in impolite company, and you may be given directions for where to get your head examined. It's a joke, right? There never was such a place, with talking snakes and paradise walks, surely? On the other hand, the respected Old Testament scholar E.A. Speiser has commented: 'Although the Paradise of the Bible was manifestly a place of mystery, its physical setting cannot be dismissed offhand as sheer imagination. To the writer of the account in Genesis 2:8ff... the Garden of Eden was obviously a reality.'[5] Explorers like Marco Polo attempted to find the garden somewhere in the Mongolian borders, and early Jewish thinkers thought it might be in India. Some today think it lies near or under the Persian Gulf.

For the Bible, however, the big story about Eden is that it has been lost! Indeed, for the writer of Genesis, the significance of the events of the fall (Genesis 3) and the subsequent flood (Genesis 6) is that the world now is not as it was then. There remains in the human heart a sort of racial memory, captured in many cultures, of a paradise now lost. Poignantly and wistfully, C.S. Lewis expressed the feeling of nostalgia as 'only the scent of a flower we have not found, the echo of a tune we have not heard, news from a country we have never yet visited'.[6] Now, between humankind and that garden stands 'a flaming sword flashing back and forth to guard the way to the tree of life' (v. 24). Is there no way back into that lost paradise?

The overarching story of the rest of the Bible is that there is. But there are many wrong roads and bypath meadows until paradise is restored and we are given 'the right to eat from the tree of life, which is in the paradise of God' (Revelation 2:7). One of those detours is encountered in our reading: 'Cain was then building a city, and he named it after his son Enoch' (v. 17). Although there will be more positive nuances for the word later in the Bible's story, the first mention of 'city' here is negative. It begins to lay the groundwork for what city often comes to symbolise: life without God; life outside Eden; life lived my way, where I, like Cain, name things after my family or myself.

By the time we read Psalm 55, we are beginning to see how negative the metaphor of the city has become:

Lord, confuse the wicked, confound their words,
for I see violence and strife in the city.
Day and night they prowl about on its walls;
malice and abuse are within it.

Destructive forces are at work in the city;
threats and lies never leave its streets.
PSALM 55: 9–11

Deep in the Israelites' history and heart lay the pain of their beloved city Jerusalem, the putative 'joy of the whole earth' (Psalm 48:2), reduced to ashes and mourned in the words of Lamentations after its destruction by Babylon: 'they scoff and shake their heads at Daughter Jerusalem: "Is this the city that was called the perfection of beauty, the joy of the whole earth?"' (Lamentations 2:15). Life without God is tough, that is the message. And somewhere deep within our hearts is an emptiness that longs to be filled again with the divine presence. There is in the human spirit a longing and desire to find peace and security from the din of the city and the bustle of the world. Where is it found?

First aired on British TV in 2002, *Escape to the Country* continues to the present day. The basic idea of the programme is that an individual or family wishes to relocate and find a peaceful, rural retreat from the hustle and bustle of their city life. The show is appropriately named. In contrast, Christians are not called to be escapists, at least in the accepted sense of the term. But the combined story of the birth, life, death and resurrection of Jesus is a clarion call and offer to 'Escape to Christ', and paradoxically find our place in this world and subsequently the next.

Monday

....

Superheroes or villains?

When human beings began to increase in number on the earth and daughters were born to them, the sons of God saw that the daughters of humans were beautiful, and they married any of them they chose. Then the Lord said, 'My Spirit will not contend with humans forever, for they are mortal; their days will be a hundred and twenty years.'

The Nephilim were on the earth in those days – and also afterward – when the sons of God went to the daughters of humans and had children by them. They were the heroes of old, men of renown.

The Lord saw how great the wickedness of the human race had become on the earth, and that every inclination of the thoughts of the human heart was only evil all the time. The Lord regretted that he had made human beings on the earth, and his heart was deeply troubled. So the Lord said, 'I will wipe from the face of the earth the human race I have created – and with them the animals, the birds and the creatures that move along the ground – for I regret that I have made them.' But Noah found favour in the eyes of the Lord.

GENESIS 6:1–8

The simplest way to interpret this passage is that the 'sons of God' in verse 2 are either human beings in the line of Seth (Genesis 5:3, 6) or are 'men of renown' (v. 4), that is, powerful rulers or 'sons of the Most High' (Psalm 82:6). If the former, then Seth's sons are beginning to interbreed with some ungodly line. If the latter, then here are despotic rulers, perhaps brutally abducting women to their harems ('they married any of them they chose', v. 2). This has many modern parallels: think of those fleeing the atrocities of so-called Islamic State.

Yet another possibility, with a long history of interpretation, ancient and modern, is that we are being reminded of something – and I use the word advisedly – 'alien' being introduced into the human race, the 'sons of God' being some form of non-human spiritual beings who seek directly to infiltrate and interfere with humanity. That would be strange indeed, and is often dismissed as some form of primeval fiction on a par with the introduction to *Star Wars*: 'A long time ago in a galaxy far, far away...'

Before we totally dismiss the idea, we would do well to recall that for the Bible dark and sinister powers do exist. Some interpreters think there are recurring biblical reminiscences of something mysterious, hideous and catastrophic in our history (see, for example, 1 Peter 3:19; 2 Peter 2:4; Jude 6; Revelation 12:7–9). Indeed, many cultures seem to dimly echo threats to humanity from dark, sophisticated and bent-on-evil powers that are beyond the human.

Be that as it may, the warning here is that humanity can cross a forbidden line in its quest for fame and immortality of the kind that is independent of the living God. That is the possible meaning of 'My spirit will not remain in humans' (v. 3, NIV footnote). Earthly life has its limits. Methuselah might be 969 when he dies (Genesis 5:27), but life has its boundaries, whether it is Moses' 120 years (Deuteronomy 34:7) or the psalmist's 'three score and ten' years allotted to most of us (Psalm 90:10).

So, the actions of these sons of God result in the Nephilim, some form of superior beings, 'men of renown' (v. 4). Welcome to their brave new world. The lure of what we now call eugenics, the creation of a master race, did not originate with Adolf Hitler or his imitators. Unfortunately, superpowers wielded by fallen human beings, ancient and modern, are a recipe for catastrophe. In this case, the flood ensues (vv. 5–7).

Edward Lorenz was a meteorologist and mathematician working in the 1960s on computer modelling for weather systems at the Massachusetts Institute of Technology. One day, when intending to enter a six-decimal-place number he inserted only three decimal places instead. His intuition told him that, as it was an inconsequential amount, it would not make much difference. But he was wrong, for it revised the weather forecast dramatically. It was as if a tiny atmospheric disturbance in Beijing, no larger than a butterfly moving its wing, had a week later given rise to a force 12 hurricane battering New York. This led to the principle now known as the butterfly effect, an insignificant event having undreamed-of consequences.

Something like that effect is at work in Genesis 3 and in this narrative. Humanity's disconnection from God's original design has increased to a point where, if left unchecked, it will be beyond hope and repair. How near is the impending judgement of the flood, and how far away from the city of God. A new start is needed.

And such is at hand: 'But Noah found favour in the eyes of the Lord... a righteous man... he walked faithfully with God' (vv. 8–9). Regress and progress for humanity beckons! An ark of salvation is prepared, the fulfilment of which will be the coming of one whose death and resurrection will be the ultimate butterfly effect, leading to salvation for the world. A real superhero is coming!

Tuesday

....

Human potential and its hubris

Now the whole world had one language and a common speech. As people moved eastward, they found a plain in Shinar and settled there.

They said to each other, 'Come, let's make bricks and bake them thoroughly.' They used brick instead of stone, and bitumen for mortar. Then they said, 'Come, let us build ourselves a city, with a tower that reaches to the heavens, so that we may make a name for ourselves; otherwise we will be scattered over the face of the whole earth.'

But the Lord came down to see the city and the tower the people were building. The Lord said, 'If as one people speaking the same language they have begun to do this, then nothing they plan to do will be impossible for them. Come, let us go down and confuse their language so they will not understand each other.'

So the Lord scattered them from there over all the earth, and they stopped building the city. That is why it was called Babel – because there the Lord confused the language of the whole world. From there the Lord scattered them over the face of the whole earth.

GENESIS 11:1–9

'He were a big lad', as they say in Yorkshire. Over six-feet tall, he towered over me after the morning service at which I had spoken in his home city of Ripon. 'So, you come from Liverpool, lad?' he enquired. 'I do.' 'Well,' he said, 'there are only three types of people in the world: those born in Yorkshire; those who wish they were born in Yorkshire; and those with no ambition at all!'

Who wants to disagree with a bloke that big? We both laughed. But beyond the humour, the world is sharply divided by those who think they know better and feel superior to others – and are delighted to let the rest of us know it too!

Say what you will about the fabled Babel, those folks certainly had no problems when it came to self-image and self-promotion: 'Come, let us build ourselves a city, with a tower that reaches to the heavens, so that we may make a name for ourselves.' Here is one of the great birthplaces of pride, a palace of human hubris. And the word 'hubris' is appropriate here. In ancient Greek, from which the word is derived, hubris is the attitude that defies the gods, does its own thing and inevitably leads to catastrophe. It is closely linked to the more familiar word pride. Of course, we all smile at the child who is blissfully unaware of their limitations and, after painfully picking out 'Chopsticks' on a keyboard for Grandma, thinks he now possesses outstanding musical ability. Such pride we indulge; perhaps in due time it will give birth to some necessary self-esteem and realism. But the hubris and pride on display in Babel is not to be smiled at: it is self-confident, self-reliant, utterly self-sufficient and God-denying. The words of William Ernest Henley's 'Invictus' ('Unconquered'), whatever their original intent, illustrate it graphically:

> It matters not how strait the gate,
> How charged with punishments the scroll,
> I am the master of my fate,
> I am the captain of my soul.[7]

What is both alarming and so contemporary about Babel is its undoubted abilities. Here is the fount of utopian dreams, of conquest of the universe, of proud empires and of people for whom 'nothing will be impossible'. An exaggeration perhaps? Hardly, for that is God's verdict on their human ingenuity and potential (v. 6). Babel operated with the amorality of much of today's world: if it can be done, it should be done, regardless of the moral issues involved.

The application of this 'Babel principle' is of pressing urgency in our world today. On the one hand, we rightly applaud human ingenuity and can be grateful for the massive strides in science that can put a person on the moon and provide the medicine that saves a child's life. I am writing this chapter in Japan, on the other side of the world from where I live, thankful that it took only twelve hours to reach here and a mere twelve seconds to call my wife on my mobile phone. Christians are not called to be Luddites! On the other hand, the vast scale of deforestation, the excess burning of fossil fuels, the pollution of our seas and the threat of nuclear disaster by accident or terror threatens life on the planet. If it can be done, the moral question is should it? We may attempt to build towers that reach to the heavens, announcing our new world order. Who or what is going to stop us? But what happens when those towers turn out to be castles in the air that crash to earth with devastating effect?

Here, of course, there was direct, divine intervention: 'the Lord scattered them' (v. 8). The confusion of the Esperanto of the day into a myriad of tongues was designed for human protection – to preserve humanity from one of its greatest enemies, itself. Otherwise, holocausts, gulags and killing fields would be the order of every day and not just huge blots on humanity's history page.

However, one day, in another city, Jerusalem, the confusion of tongues, the divisions of humanity, and the life of independence from the living God would again be addressed. Whatever else is involved in the phenomenon of 'speaking in tongues' on the day of Pentecost, here was a marker set down by God that a new day had dawned: '"How is it that each of us hears them in our native language? … we hear them declaring the wonders of God in our own tongues!" Amazed and perplexed, they asked one another, "What does this mean?"' (Acts 2:8–12). Peter tells them: through the life, death, resurrection and ascension of Jesus, a world-changing moment has arrived to cure humanity's hubris. In the light of Christ's coming another question should arise: 'What shall we do?' The answer: 'Repent and be baptised, every one of you, in the name of

Jesus Christ for the forgiveness of your sins. And you will receive the gift of the Holy Spirit' (Acts 2:37–38). Babel's curse is being reversed, and humanity's potential is to be rediscovered not in independence from God but dependence upon him and his Son through the gift of his Spirit.

Wednesday

A saved soul and a wasted life

With the coming of dawn, the angels urged Lot, saying, 'Hurry! Take your wife and your two daughters who are here, or you will be swept away when the city is punished.'

When he hesitated, the men grasped his hand and the hands of his wife and of his two daughters and led them safely out of the city, for the Lord was merciful to them. As soon as they had brought them out, one of them said, 'Flee for your lives! Don't look back, and don't stop anywhere in the plain! Flee to the mountains or you will be swept away!'

By the time Lot reached Zoar, the sun had risen over the land. Then the Lord rained down burning sulphur on Sodom and Gomorrah – from the Lord out of the heavens. Thus he overthrew those cities and the entire plain, destroying all those living in the cities – and also the vegetation in the land. But Lot's wife looked back, and she became a pillar of salt.

GENESIS 19:15–16, 23–26

It is sometimes fun to play word-association games. You know the sort of thing: black–white; good–bad; king–queen. My grandchildren might add: grandad–sweets. If you try it with 'Lot's wife', even the biblically uninformed are likely to come up with 'pillar of salt', though any word association with 'Sodom' would today probably be met, depending on the company you are in, with awkwardness and embarrassment.

Lest we think that Sodom should be consigned to some corner of supposed Old Testament fable, it is well to be reminded that Jesus himself sternly spoke of it being 'more bearable for Sodom on the day of judgment' than for some of his contemporary cities (Matthew 11:24). And, pulling no punches, the apostle Peter adds that it was a place where Lot, a righteous man, both lived and 'was distressed by the depraved conduct of the lawless' (2 Peter 2:7). So how did Lot end up in such a place so far from the city his uncle Abram was seeking? If we needed a reason to consider him, it might be this: the possibility of experiencing 'a saved soul and a wasted life', one marked out by compromise with the world around him. There are several tributaries feeding into that conclusion.

Lot was a man of faith, for he went along with Abram's journey into the unknown: 'So Abram went, as the Lord had told him; and Lot went with him' (Genesis 12:4; see also 13:1, 5). But, just as it is easy to have a *second-hand* faith inherited from one's parents that never transforms the individual, so it is possible to have a *second-rate* faith. Lot's faith was genuine – he is called 'a righteous man' (2 Peter 2:7) – but his life was characterised by choosing the soft option. When conflict arose, in Genesis 13, and different directions were possible, he moved 'towards the east' (v. 11). The significance of this 'theological geography' is easy to miss: not only does he end up 'near Sodom' (v. 12), but it runs counter to the westerly direction in which Abram was travelling, towards the promised land! Before long, Lot is not only near but 'living in' Sodom (14:12). And by the time he is miraculously rescued from it, 'Lot was sitting in the gateway of the city' (19:1), an ancient marker of being in a place of influence.

The events recorded in Genesis 19 are intended to shock us deeply. He is not only in Sodom, Sodom and its depravity has seeped into him. How else can we explain his wickedness in offering his two virgin daughters to the sexual predators at his door in order to protect his visitors? The daughters' subsequent reprehensible actions in getting their father drunk and committing incest with him (vv. 30–38) can only be mitigated by the indelible impression left on them during that unforgettable occasion, as they were offered up as sexual playthings.

In many areas of life, we can all mess up. Like Lot, it is possible to choose the easy option and take the path leading from the high road of faith to the undulating, low road of doubt. But what do we do when 'the city' we have chosen for ourselves begins to crumble or, like Sodom, faces imminent destruction? On that dreadful night of Sodom's demise, Lot was rescued by angelic intervention because of his uncle, who sought the face of God for mercy (Genesis 18). On the road to Easter, we need to pause and thank God for the one who prayed, 'Father, forgive them, for they do not know what they are doing' (Luke 23:34).

Does that mean we should just carry on, ignoring the warning signs of danger to our families or ourselves? Recall that Lot's choices had consequences. His grandchildren, Moab and Ammon, became a thorn in the side of Israel's subsequent history. And, unlike Abraham, who continues to have a leading role in the biblical story in both testaments, Lot's name disappears from the biblical narrative until our Lord warns us, 'Remember Lot's wife!' (Luke 17:32).

Yes, a saved soul and a wasted life. Lot's legacy! Pray it won't be ours.

Thursday

....

A place for tears

Sarah lived to be a hundred and twenty-seven years old. She died at Kiriath Arba (that is, Hebron) in the land of Canaan, and Abraham went to mourn for Sarah and to weep over her.

Then Abraham rose from beside his dead wife and spoke to the Hittites. He said, 'I am a foreigner and stranger among you. Sell me some property for a burial site here so I can bury my dead.'

Abraham agreed to Ephron's terms and weighed out for him the price he had named in the hearing of the Hittites: four hundred shekels of silver, according to the weight current among the merchants.

So Ephron's field in Machpelah near Mamre – both the field and the cave in it, and all the trees within the borders of the field – was legally made over to Abraham as his property in the presence of all the Hittites who had come to the gate of the city. Afterwards Abraham buried his wife Sarah in the cave in the field of Machpelah near Mamre (which is at Hebron) in the land of Canaan. So the field and the cave in it were legally made over to Abraham by the Hittites as a burial site.

GENESIS 23:1–4, 16–20

'Death has climbed in through our windows and has entered our fortresses' is the graphic way the prophet Jeremiah describes the one great certainty of life (Jeremiah 9:21). Whether it comes through the windows, doors or sewers into the dwelling of our lives, arrive it will. Its statistics are most impressive, according to a quip by George Bernard Shaw: 'one out of one people die'. As I am writing this, I am trying to contact a relative whose husband woke up fighting for breath during the night, and was gone before the ambulance arrived. Every day in every generation, the great drama predicted back in Genesis is played out, 'dying you shall die' (2:17, literal translation).

Abraham may be on his way to his perceived promised land but his life partner, Sarah, will not be there to enjoy it with him. Here's a lesser-known city we'll all visit sooner or later, Kiriath Arba. And some of us today are still red-raw with grief after visiting there with a loved one whom we had to leave behind, whether yesterday or years ago. Grief has many guises and disguises, and is as long as a piece of string. It is shortened or lengthened by many factors. How do we cope when Kiriath Arba beckons? May Abraham's example, with a few additions to it, turn us to the God who 'heals the broken-hearted and binds up their wounds' (Psalm 147:3).

Be thankful

What a life Sarah and Abraham had shared. Indeed, the Hebrew idiom here in the text speaks about the '*lives* of Sarah' (v. 1). I suspect when you have lived to 127 that's one way to put it! She had set out with Abram on a journey of faith (Genesis 11:31), and had almost ended up not once but twice in some potentate's harem (12:14–20; 20:1–18). Then, at 90, she'd given birth to a son (21:1–7). Like any life, it was not perfect, for neither was she. Her advice that Abram should sleep with her maid, Hagar, and the cruelty it subsequently provoked (16:1–16; 21:8–21) are not glossed over in the Bible. We are wise not to canonise in death our loved ones, as if they were perfect, even though they were wonderful to us.

Be tearful

One of the positive elements to have entered our funeral culture in recent years is the note of celebration, the opportunity to be grateful for a loved one's life. What is concerning to some of us who conduct such events is that the bereaved are almost discouraged from grieving at all. We emphasise the departed's accomplishments, we smile at their foibles and we send them off with a blast of Frank Sinatra's version of 'My Way'. In contrast, Abraham 'went to mourn for Sarah and to weep over her' (v. 2). This was not because he had no hope, or did not know about some form of life after death. Rather, as Paul reminds the Thessalonians, it was OK to grieve, but not 'like the rest of mankind, who have no hope' (1 Thessalonians 4:13). After all, at the death of Lazarus, the Lord Jesus himself wept (John 11:35). But why the grief if we 'go to heaven when we die'? Because the Bible views death as an unlawful intruder who robs us of life. It is still 'the last enemy' (1 Corinthians 15:26), though it is not the last word – Christ is! Tears are important in the grief process.

Be resourceful

In death, there is a great deal to be done by the living, as this chapter amply demonstrates. Abraham needs to negotiate with Ephron the Hittite for a burial site. The oriental customs involved, alien to many of us, of bargaining over the price, discreetly mentioned, may mean Abraham paid 'over the odds' (vv. 10–16). On the other hand, we are acting wisely when we prepare in life for what we wish for in death. It has been my privilege to carry out, sometimes scrupulously, the wishes of the departed in terms of hymns chosen, things to say, passages to read – and people to avoid! Thoughtful planning, clear communication, and the valuing of the opportunity that one's funeral may present are to be commended.

Be hopeful

It would be a mistake to leave this chapter concluding that it is an ancient version of how to pre-plan a funeral. Let's notice that the passage is topped and tailed by an electrifying word in its context,

Canaan (vv. 2, 19). This is what Abraham's journeying is about. Although he is 'a foreigner and stranger' (v. 4), he now has a foothold and a grave in the promised land! It is not, to be sure, the Holy City, but it is a marker on the way, even in death, of the promise of life. In laying Sarah's remains to rest Abraham, in a way yet to be explained, is anticipating the fulfilment of the promise of the one who says, 'a time is coming and has now come when the dead will hear the voice of the Son of God and those who hear will live', even those in the grave (John 5:25, 28). Christians are to face death, acknowledging both its pain and horror, while thanking God for Jesus, the resurrection and the life!

....

Mid-life crisis

After a long time Judah's wife, the daughter of Shua, died. When Judah had recovered from his grief, he went up to Timnah, to the men who were shearing his sheep, and his friend Hirah the Adullamite went with him.

When Tamar was told, 'Your father-in-law is on his way to Timnah to shear his sheep,' she took off her widow's clothes, covered herself with a veil to disguise herself, and then sat down at the entrance to Enaim...

When Judah saw her, he thought she was a prostitute, for she had covered her face. Not realising that she was his daughter-in-law, he went over to her by the roadside and said, 'Come now, let me sleep with you.'

... and she became pregnant by him.

About three months later Judah was told, 'Your daughter-in-law Tamar is guilty of prostitution, and as a result she is now pregnant.' Judah said, 'Bring her out and let her be burned to death!'

As she was being brought out, she sent a message to her father-in-law. 'I am pregnant by the man who owns these,' she said. And she added, 'See if you recognise whose seal and cord and staff these are.'

Judah recognised them and said, 'She is more righteous than I, since I wouldn't give her to my son Shelah.' And he did not sleep with her again.

GENESIS 38:12–18, 24–26

A friend of mine, a management consultant, was delivering some hard facts to a failing company. The air bristled, but he always had his stock reply ready: 'I'm only the postman delivering the mail.' There are times when we discover unpalatable stuff in our Bibles and here's a case in point. Scripture is not holding up this story for a 'go and do likewise' application. Rather, it is reporting the state of the company, in this instance one of Jacob's sons, Judah. If the previous chapter of Genesis was intensely shocking as Joseph, another of Jacob's sons, was sold off into slavery, narrowly avoiding being murdered by his brothers, this one is likewise scandalous. It might be called 'How to grow old *dis*gracefully'. Here's a pilgrim in definite regress!

Later in Genesis and in the unfolding biblical story, Judah and his name will be forever remembered, as through his tribe the long-promised King, mirrored in David and fulfilled in Jesus, is to come and establish his kingdom. Here, however, all that is a distant prospect. Although we are not given his age, it's fair to assume he's hit mid-life – and a crisis! How did he get there?

Some bad choices

At last, Judah leaves home, and the trouble begins. He goes 'down' and then teams up with a pal, Hirah, who seems to be a matchmaker, for Judah meets and marries a woman whose name is not given but whose background is 'a Canaanite' (vv. 1–3). Unlike the standoffish Egyptians we later encounter in Genesis, the Canaanites were friendly. Like many young people pushing off to university or a job away from home, Judah enters a vulnerable period where he forgets, if he ever remembered, that his family were to be part of the big story to bring salvation to the world. So, he goes ahead and marries outside his faith community, unlike his grandfather and dad (see Genesis 24; 29).

When tragedy strikes

Initially, all seems well and three sons are born. Significantly, the last one is delivered in a place called Kezib – the town of deception, a theme that runs through the chapter. Tragedy strikes with the death of his two older sons, the details of which won't detain us here (though see Deuteronomy 25:5–6 for the custom of levirate marriage, a brother-in-law's marriage to a childless widow). Now Judah begins to suspect that his daughter-in-law is bad luck, and is reluctant for his third son to go the way of the other two (v. 11). Then, further tragedy: his wife dies, and grief sets in.

Uncontrollable consequences

It is very easy to underestimate our weaknesses. Like Judah, we can make mistakes in our younger years and we go 'down' (v. 1). Later, we assume we've learned our lesson. But Judah's biggest mess-up occurred when he was much older and went 'up' to Timnah, as his grief began to lift (v. 12). Tamar, misled by him, seizes her opportunity to deceive him (v. 14). Whether she detected some sexual vulnerability in her father-in-law or was merely opportunistic, the resulting narrative is almost comical while also deeply shocking. It is comical in that Judah was so easily deceived; he is neither the first nor the last to lose his reputation with a sex worker. It is a commentary and indictment on our times that the prevalence of sexually transmitted diseases has grown massively, not only among the young but also among much older people. But the truly deplorable elements here are the display of double standards and male chauvinism at its worst. When Tamar's pregnancy is discovered, Judah orders her to be burned to death (v. 24). Thankfully, she produces a 'get out of jail free' card – three of them, in fact (v. 25). To his credit, Judah comes clean and stays that way (v. 26).

Amazing grace

Is this narrative, then, just a piece of ancient voyeuristic tabloid journalism from this 'town of lies'? Hardly. It is one of the building blocks for why Jacob and his family needed to get out of the promised land of Canaan (Genesis 37:1), so that they might eventually re-enter a better country. What is remarkable is the appearance, centuries later, of Tamar, along with Judah and her two sons, as they are cited in the genealogy of Jesus (Matthew 1:3). There's a well-known hymn being played as the melodious background music to this cacophony of human intrigue, sexual failure and deceit – 'Amazing Grace'. For the abiding truth is that it is grace that saves 'a wretch' like Judah. The Lord tolerates and bears with human sin and failure not because he intends to ignore and forget it. Rather, his great design is to forgive and redeem humanity from its 'city of lies' one day in Jerusalem.

Saturday

···

Eisodus comes before exodus

Then Joseph brought his father Jacob in and presented him before Pharaoh. After Jacob blessed Pharaoh, Pharaoh asked him, 'How old are you?'

And Jacob said to Pharaoh, 'The years of my pilgrimage are a hundred and thirty. My years have been few and difficult, and they do not equal the years of the pilgrimage of my fathers.' Then Jacob blessed Pharaoh and went out from his presence.

So Joseph settled his father and his brothers in Egypt and gave them property in the best part of the land, the district of Rameses, as Pharaoh directed.

Jacob lived in Egypt seventeen years, and the years of his life were a hundred and forty-seven. When the time drew near for Israel to die, he called for his son Joseph and said to him, 'If I have found favour in your eyes, put your hand under my thigh and promise that you will show me kindness and faithfulness. Do not bury me in Egypt, but when I rest with my fathers, carry me out of Egypt and bury me where they are buried.'

'I will do as you say,' he said.

'Swear to me,' he said. Then Joseph swore to him, and Israel worshipped as he leaned on the top of his staff.

GENESIS 47:7–11, 28–31

An elderly gentleman was being shown around a retirement home and was rather resistant to the idea of becoming a resident. 'Well,' said the kindly matron, 'there is a little test we use to help you assess whether you do in fact need the support our home offers.' She took him to one of the bathrooms, where there was a bath full of water, a sink, a toilet and a bucket next to the bath. 'What is the quickest way to empty the bath?' she asked. 'Easy! I'd keep filling the bucket and emptying it down the toilet till the job's done!' he replied rather triumphantly. 'No, it isn't, Mr Smith. The easiest way to empty the bath is to remove the plug. We have a delightful room for you on the first floor.'

Let's be honest, it's no fun for many of us as our years increase. Here's Jacob having to make a huge transition when he is 130 years old (v. 9), after learning that the son he thought was dead was wonderfully alive (45:25–28). Is this, then, an encouraging narrative on how to prepare for old age? Certainly, and there are moral and spiritual lessons galore in these later chapters of Genesis on families and how to survive them! But the major focus is elsewhere. Most Christians know about the *exodus*, Israel's coming out of Egypt; these chapters introduce us to the *eisodus*, how Israel got into Egypt.

Why was Israel in Egypt in the first place? Hadn't they already arrived in Canaan, the promised land? Geographically, they had, but spiritually, they were a long way from home. We read of family breakdowns, cover-ups, rape, adultery, prostitution, murder and narrowly avoided fratricide! Is this what God's kingdom is to look like, mimicking the Canaanite morals all around them? How will 'all peoples ... be blessed' through Abraham and his progeny (Genesis 12:3) when they are part of the problem? Sometimes, a failing school is put into 'special measures' to improve it. Egypt will become those special measures for Jacob and his family so that, almost totally quarantined from pagan influences, they have their own space in Goshen to grow into a great nation (Exodus 1:9).

To effect that eisodus, there are the intriguing ways of God. Enter Joseph, who dominates these later chapters. When we first meet him (Genesis 37) he is the kid brother, the dreamer and his father's favourite (always a mistake!). He quickly goes from being something of a somebody, with that flashy coat, to slavery, being falsely accused of attempted rape, and prison. Then remarkably, in a short space of time he becomes the prime minister in Egypt. Later, when Joseph's brothers fear that he will take his revenge after their father's death, Joseph reminds them: 'You intended to harm me, but God intended it for good to accomplish what is now being done, the saving of many lives' (Genesis 50:20). Their wickedness is not excused but sovereignly overseen and overcome to bring blessing to them and ultimately the world. Joseph, the son so loved by his father, hated by his brothers, suffered for no crime, was presumed dead, then exalted to a throne to reign as his people's saviour. He preserved them through and beyond the famine. It is the pattern of a righteous sufferer, echoed in other Old Testament characters like Job and Jeremiah. Supremely, there's the elusive, enigmatic servant who suffers and dies, lamb-like, for his people and their transgressions, yet justifies many, bringing them peace and healing, as he becomes 'highly exalted' (Isaiah 52:13—53:12).

Such characters, along with Joseph, the 'ruler of all Egypt' (45:8), are types and shadows, anticipating events recorded at Easter, Pentecost and beyond: the great reversals of suffering to triumph, of death to life. In the first 'Christian' sermon, Peter says:

> *This man was handed over to you by God's deliberate plan and foreknowledge; and you, with the help of wicked men, put him to death by nailing him to the cross. But God raised him from the dead, freeing him from the agony of death, because it was impossible for death to keep its hold on him... Therefore let all Israel be assured of this: God has made this Jesus, whom you crucified, both Lord and Messiah.*
> ACTS 2:23–24, 36

My opening paragraph was not intended to be completely facetious. Are you facing a major challenge and a possible move, and resisting it? It might be forced on you because of your job, a relational breakdown or, mirroring Jacob, your increasing years. God may have 'a delightful room' for you. Jacob enjoyed Joseph for 17 years, lost him for a couple of decades or more, and had him back for his final 17 years (Genesis 37:2; 47:9, 28). Nothing vital is ever lost when surrendered to the Lord. God intended it all for good. By the way, how did you get on with the bathroom test? Come on, be honest!

Week 2

....

Finding a home: undulating experiences of God

In the Psalms the soul turns inwards on itself, and their great feature is that they are the expression of a large spiritual experience. They come straight from the heart, and the secret depths of the spirit.
Dean Church[8]

I first encountered this week's comparatively short psalms as a 15-year-old, after I had climbed what I thought was the Everest of the Bible's chapters, Psalm 119, with its 176 verses, and thinking it would never conclude. At that time, the songs of degrees or ascents, Psalms 120—134, felt like I had time to draw breath after running up the mountain of Psalm 119. Their title probably derives from their being sung by Jewish pilgrims as they went up to worship at the main Jewish festivals of Passover, Pentecost and Tabernacles. So they were originally composed for people on a journey from their own towns, villages and hamlets to the great city of God, Jerusalem.

Today's people of God are pilgrims too, on a journey from this world to the great city of God, the heavenly Jerusalem. This week we journey through some of the mountaintop and valley experiences of the pilgrim's way.

Sunday

·····································

Everybody needs good neighbours

I call on the Lord in my distress,
  and he answers me.
Save me, Lord,
  from lying lips
  and from deceitful tongues.
What will he do to you,
  and what more besides,
  you deceitful tongue?
He will punish you with a warrior's sharp arrows,
  with burning coals of the broom bush.
Woe to me that I dwell in Meshek,
  that I live among the tents of Kedar!
Too long have I lived
  among those who hate peace.
I am for peace;
  but when I speak, they are for war.

PSALM 120

The Australian soap opera *Neighbours* first aired over 30 years ago, and continues to draw huge audiences as it cleverly portrays the strengths and challenges of life in Ramsay Street, a small cul-de-sac in the fictional suburb of Erinsborough, in Melbourne. Many of us experience both the joys of good neighbours and, like this psalm, the difficulties of bad ones, whether we live in a city, town or village.

Clearly, the psalmist is struggling with both his location and his neighbours: 'Woe to me that I dwell in Meshek and Kedar' (see

Genesis 10:2; 25:13), which suggests that he feels a long way from home. He is dislocated; he does not belong where he finds himself. Moreover, his references to lies, deceit and war suggest that his neighbours are as fierce, cruel and hard to please as the worst barbarians he can imagine; a modern-day analogy might be the so-called Islamic State. Accordingly, because of his deep faith, he feels like a fish out of water, being personally peaceable while his neighbours are always up for a fight (vv. 6–7).

His desire for peace, however, does not cloud his judgement when he is living among people who lie and deceive. It is easy to fall into the trap of thinking that words are not important, as in the phrase 'it is what's in the heart that counts'. The Bible's view is rather different. Words are immensely powerful, being one of the indicators of what is going on in our hearts. Recall our Lord's statement that 'the mouth speaks what the heart is full of' (Luke 6:45). Indeed, according to Jesus, by our words we may be either 'acquitted or condemned' (Matthew 12:37). So, verses 3 and 4 anticipate such judgement as the psalmist expresses, in colourful language, the consequences and cost of lying.

The motto of the London Stock Exchange, in use for hundreds of years, is *Dictum Meum Pactum*, 'My word is my bond'. Behind that is the conviction that integrity, and the keeping of one's promises, are essential for good business practice. Words matter. The psalmist's complaint is that they clearly don't count for much with his neighbours. Sadly, lies and treachery are everyday occurrences in business, politics, neighbourhoods, families and individuals. Ask the pensioner who has been scammed for her life savings, the wife who has been betrayed by her husband's infidelity, the teenager deceived into the sex trade via promises of a better life, and the child crying for a parent who promised to visit but never did.

In his distress, the psalmist turns to the Lord: 'I call on the Lord' (v. 1). Scripture constantly reminds us that our God 'is light; in him there is no darkness at all' (1 John 1:5). Christians follow one who is 'the truth' (John 14:6) and 'the one true God' (Isaiah 65:16). Such light and truth is the antithesis of all forms of deception. God is transparent. Accordingly, the prayer to be delivered 'from lying lips' needs to be applied to ourselves each day before we apply it to others (vv. 1–2).

If we have good neighbours, let's be grateful for them. If we have bad ones, take a leaf out of the psalmist's book and bring them to the Lord in prayer. Meanwhile, let's aim to be a 'good Samaritan' neighbour if we can!

Monday

....

Upwardly mobile

I lift up my eyes to the mountains –
    where does my help come from?
My help comes from the Lord,
    the Maker of heaven and earth.
He will not let your foot slip –
    he who watches over you will not slumber;
indeed, he who watches over Israel
    will neither slumber nor sleep.
The Lord watches over you –
    The Lord is your shade at your right hand;
the sun will not harm you by day,
    nor the moon by night.
The Lord will keep you from all harm –
    he will watch over your life;
the Lord will watch over your coming and going
    both now and for evermore.

PSALM 121

Not long after 9/11, as I passed through an American airport, I knew what friends meant by a feeling of Fortress America. Questions, shoes off, bags scanned, passport examined and so on. It was understandable given the threat from global terrorism. However, it is easy to lose perspective about security issues. Are we the first generation to be conscious of such? Hardly, as this psalm makes clear. Protection was a burning issue for any would-be pilgrim taking a journey up to Jerusalem. We need only recall our Lord's parable about the good Samaritan, in which a man falls victim to thieves who leave him for dead. Throughout history, security has been a constant problem for human beings. Here we note the psalmist lifting his eyes to the hills, knowing that they stand between him and his goal of reaching Jerusalem.

Journeys undertaken, whether literal or metaphorical on the road of faith, are always potentially threatening. Many of us become conscious, especially as we age, of our weaknesses, both physically and spiritually. We may begin to echo the words of an old hymn by George Duffield (1818–88), 'the arm of flesh will fail you'. So how do we make it through the journey of life, staying full of faith and courage?

Despite his perplexity, the writer directs our attention to the power of God (v. 2). Human beings were never created to be self-sufficient. Realising that, our helplessness is one of the great aids to discovering God's aid, since he is indeed 'an ever-present help in trouble' (Psalm 46:1). Is that help enough? Of course! The Lord is 'the maker of heaven and earth', the creator of all, as the story of the Bible from Genesis (1:1) to Revelation (4:11) emphasises. God's omnipotence, his all-powerfulness as creator and sustainer of life, is always the answer to human weakness and despair. As one writer puts it, 'Here is living help: primary, personal, wise, immeasurable.'[9]

Does that mean we don't need others' help? A chorus I used to sing as a teenager suggested so: 'If you know the Lord, you need nobody else to see you through the darkest night.' It's a nice sentiment, but rather contrary to the psalmist's experience and the Bible's overall teaching. 'May he not suffer your foot to be moved; may he who keeps you not slumber' is one way to translate verse 3, making it a wish-prayer of blessing from those around us. There is always the possibility and danger that a pilgrim may fall (Psalm 38:16). Of course, the Lord is able to keep you from falling (Jude 24). However, usually pilgrims need fellow pilgrims, since 'two are better than one', for 'if either of them falls down one can help the other up' (Ecclesiastes 4:9–10). In other words, we are to eschew being totally *independent*, needing no one, and embrace *interdependence*, being grateful for others and vice versa, and always staying totally *dependent* on the Lord. We were never meant to be loners on the road of life or faith. It is a long journey to Jerusalem, in its heavenly and earthly counterparts.

In verses 3–8, half a dozen times we are reminded that God watches over and keeps his people. The living God never sleeps, being inexhaustible (Isaiah 40:28), unlike the false gods who appear to need a nap and whose devotees need to wake them up to attend to their needs (1 Kings 18:27–29). God's people are never out of God's mind or sight. How encouraging is that!

Tuesday

The ideal home show

I rejoiced with those who said to me,
   'Let us go to the house of the Lord.'
Our feet are standing
   in your gates, Jerusalem.
Jerusalem is built like a city
   that is closely compacted together.
That is where the tribes go up —
   the tribes of the Lord —
to praise the name of the Lord
   according to the statute given to Israel.
There stand the thrones for judgment,
   the thrones of the house of David.
Pray for the peace of Jerusalem:
   'May those who love you be secure.
May there be peace within your walls
   and security within your citadels.'
For the sake of my family and friends,
   I will say, 'Peace be within you.'
For the sake of the house of the Lord our God,
   I will seek your prosperity.

PSALM 122

I so clearly remember the excitement of our tour bus of pilgrims as suddenly it came into sight, standing out against the dark sky. Although tensions and threats were running high, given the Gulf War, nevertheless over 30 of us had landed that late evening in Tel Aviv. Now we were approaching Jerusalem, some of us, myself included, for the first time. Marvellous! Magnificent! Mystical!

This psalm paints both an ideal and a realistic picture of the ancient city. The psalmist expresses consummate delight (v. 1) and an almost dreamlike quality of being there even before his arrival (v. 2). Part of that is because of the encouragement and fellowship he experiences from fellow believers who, like him, long to be in God's dwelling. Contrast his exuberance with the sense of dull duty that characterises much churchgoing in the West. Compare that to the anticipation of the football fan as they approach a big game for their club: the preparation, the expense, the time, the effort and the engagement when in the stadium, along with the singing, shouting, encouraging, mourning and cursing. And all with people of like mind and passion: they love their club! The psalmist loves 'the house of the Lord' (v. 9).

Jerusalem was previously Jebus (Joshua 15:63), a place of idolatry that became a place for the worship God. In this psalm, its physical unity is a metaphor for its people's unity, which nevertheless is expressed in colourful diversity – 'the tribes go up' (v. 4). God's people were never intended to be monochrome. But they are united by his truth, his 'statute given to Israel', and headed towards a city where justice and truth are found (v. 5). Our local churches are likewise intended to be such places: where the word of God is found, where his people in all their diversity gather, promoting righteousness and justice and united in the great vision of celebrating their God's greatness.

Have you ever been to the Ideal Home Show, held every year in London, or similar exhibitions? I wonder how I and my home have survived so long without the latest, time-saving gadget or design! I suspect it is possible to see such an ideal home and lose the will to live! In this psalm, truth to tell, we are likewise confronted by the ideal home. Is it over the top in its fulsome praise of Jerusalem? Jerusalem may seem to be a castle in the air. Indeed, from that direction another writer will one day see it descend (Revelation 21:2). Meanwhile, the psalmist is more realistic, and prays that his vision may become a reality. Jerusalem, literally and metaphorically, needs 'peace' and 'security', the emphasis of verses 6–9. So does each local community of Christians. Our churches need to be 'a safe place for a dangerous message', as the American pastor Bill Hybels has quipped – the place where the dangerous, life-changing message of God's outrageous grace in Christ might be experienced. And lest we think he is being totally altruistic, the psalmist's earthiness avoids that. He declares an interest, alongside his desire for God's cause to prosper (v. 9) – his 'family and friends' (v. 8).

As a father of two and grandfather to four, and having a wider network of family and friends, I likewise feel I have a vested interest in the fortunes of the community I serve and the country where I live. I believe the Lord Jesus is the best news for any individual, family, neighbourhood and land. The original motto of Glasgow, derived from St Mungo, was 'Let Glasgow flourish by the preaching of the Word' (now truncated to 'Let Glasgow flourish'). I think the psalmist would have opted for that unedited motto for Jerusalem. Flourishing by the word of God – an ideal home and community indeed!

Wednesday

Strong foundations

Those who trust in the Lord are like Mount Zion,
    which cannot be shaken but endures forever.
As the mountains surround Jerusalem,
    so the Lord surrounds his people
    both now and for evermore.
The sceptre of the wicked will not remain
    over the land allotted to the righteous,
for then the righteous might use
    their hands to do evil.
Lord, do good to those who are good,
    to those who are upright in heart.
But those who turn to crooked ways
    The Lord will banish with the evildoers.
Peace be on Israel.

PSALM 125

Years ago when I lived in East London, it became fashionable to dig out the coal cellar found under many Victorian terrace houses to provide an extra room. A couple of locals with little building experience were delighted to find as they dug down a surplus of bricks hidden under the floor. One day, the front of the house collapsed: they had dug out the footings, weakening the foundations. While, unlike this couple, many people take care to ensure their home is well underpinned, they do not take the trouble to ensure there are firm foundations for their lives. This psalm challenges us to do so.

Mount Zion (v. 1) was difficult to see from a distance. The encircling mountains offered protection and security. Likewise, those who 'trust in the Lord' should become incredibly stable and secure people. The trust here is more than affirming God's existence. The devils know and believe that (James 2:19)! Rather, believers rely on, cling to and confide in the Lord. Faith for them is an attitude of life, the lens through which they see the world. It may be called 'heart faith'. Such faith *believes God*, not just 'in God'. Come what may, it calculates that God is faithful and dependable, for he 'surrounds his people' always (v. 2). Such faith is intended to build stability and breathe security into people like us who are all too easily shaken and stirred by events in the world at large and in our personal universes.

Of course, the psalmist is not blind to the challenges of faith. There is 'the sceptre of the wicked' (v. 3) at work in his community. As I write today, a cache of cocaine with a street value of £50 million has washed up on a Norfolk beach. The news also reports that a 15-year-old boy has stabbed to death a 16-year-old youth. Are we losing the war on drugs and knife crime? Sadly, evil often appears to have the upper hand. For many people, evil itself is proof that there is no God. Not for the psalmist or the Bible generally. Faith believes that evil has a sell-by date, not only ultimately but also in the ebb and flow of life now. If evil always triumphed 'the righteous might use their hands to do evil' (v. 3), in revenge, abandoning the good fight of faith. God knows how much each one of us can bear. He promises to provide 'a way out so that [we] can endure it', and find his grace and power despite our weaknesses (1 Corinthians 10:13; 2 Corinthians 12:9).

So, we are not to 'turn to crooked ways' (v. 5) and so abandon our trust in the Lord. After all, Christians follow one upon whom 'the sceptre of the wicked fell'. They came with swords and staves to arrest him. He was subjected to a kangaroo court, a huge miscarriage of justice, and then ignominiously crucified at Skull Hill, covered in spit, welts, wounds and blood. Evil remained, it seemed, and had conquered. But the third day was coming. The Lord's death and resurrection have provided not only 'peace in Israel' (v. 5) but 'peace with God' (Romans 5:1), forever and for all who believe. The believer's third day will come too! Trust him!

Life in perspective

When the Lord restored the fortunes of Zion,
  we were like those who dreamed.
Our mouths were filled with laughter,
  our tongues with songs of joy.
Then it was said among the nations,
  'The Lord has done great things for them.'
The Lord has done great things for us,
  and we are filled with joy.
Restore our fortunes, O Lord,
  like streams in the Negev.
Those who sow with tears
  will reap with songs of joy.
Those who go out weeping,
  carrying seed to sow,
will return with songs of joy,
  carrying sheaves with them.

PSALM 126

What does 'normal' Christian experience look like? Joy, happiness, laughter, peace? Or is it tears, tragedy, weeping, setback? The answer, of course, is that it is both, as this psalm so elegantly demonstrates. Laughter and tears, joy and sorrow are braided together into a tapestry of colourful experience, through which we learn how to keep life in perspective, considering our yesterdays, todays and tomorrows.

Yesterday

Paul McCartney's 'Yesterday' poignantly remembers a better time than today, when 'troubles seemed so far away'. Similarly, the psalm recalls a better time. In fact, it was astoundingly good, off the Richter scale we might say. It is hard to pin down the specific occasion, but the writer recalls a moment of divine intervention. It might have been of the seismic type recorded in 2 Kings 19:35ff, when Jerusalem was miraculously delivered from Sennacherib's invading army. Or perhaps it is an allusion to the return from Babylonian exile, when the redeemed of the Lord entered 'Zion with singing', their heads crowned with 'everlasting joy' (Isaiah 51:11). Here, then, is a wise use of the past: recalling the mighty interventions of God. And because we are prone to forget even the Lord Jesus and his cross, the words of Christ in communion, 'Do this in remembrance of me', minister to our weakness: 'Never forget how much I have done for you!' Be grateful.

Today

It's possible to allow the past – 'the good old days' – to drown us in seas of melancholy and regret, a temptation more alluring the older we get. The psalmist does not intend to go there. Rather, he reasons that if God did great things back then, why not now? The picture he uses is evocative: the Negev (v. 4) being the dry, barren, seemingly fruitless southern Judean desert. However, when the rains arrive, flash flooding transforms what seems so moribund and dead. Dormant seeds, quickened by the rains, germinate and burst into life and colour: 'the desert shall rejoice, and blossom as the rose', the prophet asserted (Isaiah 35:1, KJV). In other words, he is praying for God's fresh intervention, what has traditionally been called 'revival', like an inrush of life when someone is resuscitated after a cardiac arrest.

In the UK and Europe today, the church often looks tired, moribund and finished. One of the joys of reading the history of the church is to see how God has sometimes so spectacularly intervened, when it looked like the show was all over. In 1736, Bishop Joseph Butler noted the public mood towards the Christian faith: 'Nothing remained but to set it up as a principal subject for mirth and ridicule.' Sound familiar? Check out the way the church is often portrayed and lampooned in the media. God often has other ideas. As Bishop Butler penned his words, revival was already underway in the USA. It would soon touch many parts of the UK in the great Methodist revival, spearheaded by George Whitfield, John Wesley and many others. If the Lord can move, as he did, upon countless thousands, is it too much to ask him to move afresh in our life, home, church and community? The prayerful plea of Isaiah, 'Oh, that you would rend the heavens and come down!' (64:1), is a great place to start. Be prayerful!

Tomorrow

From the picture of sudden revival, we are directed to the slower process of ancient Near Eastern farming. As the rains arrive late and the cold chills the bones, nevertheless the farmer, tears in his eyes (v. 5), sows his seed (v. 6). Likewise, if the good news of Jesus is to permeate the globe, as he said it would (Matthew 24:14), then seed must be scattered, as the parable of the sower reminds us (Mark 4:1–8). 'Songs of joy' (vv. 5–6) at harvest depend on an inexorable rule of life: you have to speculate to accumulate. If you want to reap, ensure that first you sow. Be hopeful.

....

Peace in the city

Blessed are all who fear the Lord,
  who walk in obedience to him.
You will eat the fruit of your labour;
  blessings and prosperity will be yours.
Your wife will be like a fruitful vine
  within your house;
your children will be like olive shoots
  round your table
Yes, this will be the blessing
  for the man blessed who fears the Lord.
May the Lord bless you from Zion;
  may you see the prosperity of Jerusalem
  all the days of your life.
May you live to see your children's children –
  peace be on Israel.

PSALM 128

It's been suggested that this psalm, in its original setting, was sung at Israelite weddings. 'A wedding song for Christians', Martin Luther called it. Others have speculated that it was written to show that the godly eventually do prosper, even when current circumstances seem against them. What it clearly demonstrates is what a life of individual godliness (vv. 1–2) may trigger. It is a beautifully balanced model of piety – the personal flowing into the family (vv. 3–4), and then overflowing into society (vv. 5–6). If not the total answer to inner-city deprivation, it does suggest priorities that the church ignores at its peril. It highlights God's family circle, comprising a *centre*, a *circle* and a *circumference*.

Centre: the individual (vv. 1–2)

The beginning of the psalm depicts the godly individual, whose 'fear' is not slavish (1 John 4:18) but filial – respect for one's creator and love for one's Father. This is demonstrated by obedience to God, walking in his ways. One of the recent debates in theological circles, although it goes back to the Reformation and far beyond, is the relationship between justifying and sanctifying grace, becoming a Christian and staying one. Imputed righteousness, getting 'right with God', through faith in Christ alone, a hallmark of the Protestant reformers' teaching, can be misunderstood. Such 'saving faith' also means being 'justified *in* Christ' (Galatians 2:17). Being *in* Christ involves an imparted righteousness. That is, the lifelong process of becoming like Jesus as the work of his Spirit gets underway in us. We come to Jesus, 'Just as I am'. However, he loves us too much to leave us as we are.

Verse 2 should not be hijacked from its context by purveyors of the so-called prosperity gospel. It is a piece of general wisdom – godliness and hard work in the providence of God often lead to prosperity. But they may not. Ask any committed Christian living on benefits since the mine or steel works were shut down years ago, or ill health, old age or tragedy struck. It is good to remember that the vast majority of our inheritance is future (Hebrews 10:32–39). Of course, in some quarters, piety, holiness and godliness appear to be synonyms for doom and gloom, morbidity and worm theology. None of that is here. Holiness and happiness are inextricably linked: 'Happy are all who fear the Lord… you shall be happy' (vv. 1–2, NEB).

Circle: the family (vv. 3–4)

'Lone Ranger' Christians may do some good. But personal godliness always needs a wider context. Otherwise it can degenerate into unhealthy, idiosyncratic and authoritarian expressions of piety. Family life is a superb test of one's degree of holiness! Two highly suggestive pictures are utilised in the psalm to describe the happy home. First, there is the delightful imagery of a wife as a 'fruitful vine' – attractive, appreciated, necessary and loved (v. 3). Second, the olive-shoot metaphor is used of children, who likewise need attention, nurture, discipline and training, around the 'table' of friendship and communication (v. 3). Like olives, they take time and patience to grow. It is misplaced optimism to expect peace in the church without harmony in the home.

But does not the foregoing seem somewhat removed from the real issues of the 'sink estates' of the UK? On the contrary. On the evening of 6 October 1985, the police officer Keith Blakelock was hacked to death on the Broadwater Farm Estate during a riot. It might seem simplistic, but the question persists: where were the parents of those rioting youths on that fateful night? Who can compute what difference a significant number of believers in such communities may promote? Fast forward over 30 years, and the seedbeds for renewed tension and violence – poor housing, unemployment, racial inequality and a lack of educational opportunity – remain, especially in many towns and cities in the north of England. Governments should rightly be concerned about the renewal of urban infrastructure. The church's task is to be concerned primarily about the regeneration of the hearts and lives of a city's inhabitants. If the church does not evangelise and 'moralise' the cities – who will? Godly individuals and families, being salt and light, are a great gift to any community.

Circumference: society (vv. 5–6)

The words 'Zion', 'Jerusalem' and 'Israel' (vv. 5–6) remind us of the social context of the life of faith. While personal piety can become inwardly focused, family life can develop its own fortress mentality, especially in the city. Heavy locks on doors and windows, women afraid to go out after dark, older people having to check with the gas company before allowing the meter reader in the door, children constantly warned not to talk to strangers and to only play directly outside or in the square 15 floors below: these are still facts of city life. Little wonder that the city is often a motif in the Bible for people in their rebellion against God (e.g. Genesis 11:1–9; Revelation 16:19). Can we reasonably expect to see not only our children but also our grandchildren (v. 6) survive and develop in such an environment?

For some the cost will inevitably be too great. Fear, exhaustion, employment opportunities and educational needs will continue to beckon Christians to the suburbs. On the other hand, it is rather hollow for Christians to demand that the government establish law and order, racial harmony, more jobs and better housing and education, and then not get personally involved in seeking change for the better for other people, whoever they are. If Christians do not model good citizenship and stand with the immigrant, the alienated, the unemployed, the badly housed and the poorly educated, who will? Suburban 'salt' rarely halts inner-city putrefaction; suburban 'light' rarely dispels urban gloom. Both are fine in themselves, but they are too far away. The incarnation of Christian individuals and families in the city is costly but Christlike (John 1:14). If it were to happen in significant numbers, 'Peace upon Israel' (v. 6) might be not just the desire of the church for urban areas but its experience too.

Saturday

···

Troubled waters

Out of the depths I cry to you, Lord;
   Lord, hear my voice.
Let your ears be attentive
   to my cry for mercy.
If you, Lord, kept a record of sins,
   Lord, who could stand?
But with you there is forgiveness,
   so that we can, with reverence, serve you.
I wait for the Lord, my whole being waits,
   and in his word I put my hope.
I wait for the Lord
   more than watchmen wait for the morning,
   more than watchmen wait for the morning.
Israel, put your hope in the Lord,
   for with the Lord is unfailing love
   and with him is full redemption.
He himself will redeem Israel
   from all their sins.

PSALM 130

I have just read a well-known Christian's regular newsletter. Very honestly he says, 'I battle discouragement and other negative things almost every day.' I hope he knows and reads this psalm regularly: 'an earnest and ardent prayer of the troubled heart', as one writer summarises it.[10]

First, it is important to remark that depression – the 'black dog', according to Winston Churchill – is a very common illness.

Antidepressants cost the UK National Health Service some £780,000 per day, or £285 million per year, according to the latest estimates.[11] Some Christians believe we should never be depressed: 'the Lord reigns', they affirm. Indeed, he does. The problem is that we fluctuate. Elijah, Jeremiah, the apostle Paul and a host of other worthy souls have experienced 'the dark night of the soul'. Indeed, our Lord himself, in the garden of Gethsemane, facing the cross, said, 'My soul is overwhelmed with sorrow to the point of death' (Mark 14:34). So, how do we cope when we feel we are at the end of our rope? Welcome to Psalm 130.

'Out of the depths' (v. 1) is an evocative phrase. It is the feeling of being in deep waters, well out of our comfort zone, and in trouble and distress. The tributaries to that flood of emotion may be many. Undoubtedly, the physical plays a huge part: general ill health, chemical imbalances, abusing our bodies, diet, sleep patterns, lack of exercise and age all contribute. Psychologically, we are not all wired the same. Some blessed souls are full-on extroverts, positive thinkers and real go-getters. A missionary working in a sun-kissed land said one of his friends was like the morning sun: once it and he rose in the morning, both shone all day! At the other extreme, some have a 'glass half-empty' temperament, who 'scorn delights and live laborious days', to quote John Milton. Most of us are somewhere in between. As the old spiritual expressed it, 'I'm sometimes up, and I'm sometimes down.'

When we have properly assessed our physical and psychological profiles, it is equally important to factor in the directly spiritual. In that context, the psalmist is aware of sin (v. 3) or iniquity (RSV). The underlying Hebrew word carries the sense of being crooked and twisted and expresses the deepest depths of human perversity. We never take God, the Bible, the Christian faith or ourselves seriously until we realise and confess that we are all part of a fallen, broken and rebellious humanity. Granted, depression *may* be caused by false guilt, and by no particular sin at all. The song 'Human' by Rag'n'Bone Man contains the lyrics, 'I'm only human after all; Don't put the blame on me.' There may be wisdom there for when we become oversensitive or when people become overbearing and put us on a guilt-trip. On the other hand, depression may be a necessary warning light, flashing on the dashboard of our conscience, that we need what the gospel offers – forgiveness (v. 4). And if such forgiveness is available for the worst depths of shame, our iniquity, then there is mercy available for sins on the surface of our lives too. Confession, we say, is good for the soul. Indeed. It may lift the dark clouds of depression if we patiently focus on the Lord and his word, as expectant as watchmen waiting for the dawn of a new day (vv. 5–6).

Accordingly, as he looks to a new day, in the final two verses, the psalmist encourages others similarly to hope in the Lord. If we have blown it with God and with others, we need to remember the answer to three questions:

- Why does God forgive? Because of his 'unfailing love' (v. 7).
- How does God forgive? Because with him there is 'full redemption' (v. 7). A ransom has been provided and paid, the content of which the New Testament will fill out with meaning: see Mark 10:45, for example.
- What does God forgive? 'All [our] sins' (v. 8).

The delightful song 'Reach Out I'll Be There' by the Four Tops (1966) promises to someone who feels they can't go on, because all their hope is gone, to be there: to shelter, comfort, care and provide all the love needed to see them through. The final line assures the distressed: 'You can always depend on me.' Of course, none of us can deliver on such a promise 24/7. The Lord can! Reach out. He'll be there.

Week 3

....

Rebuilding a ruin: unpromising situations

Growing up in post-war Liverpool, we were surrounded by what we affectionately called 'bombies' or 'de 'oller', whole tracks of ground that the Luftwaffe had inadvertently cleared, where row upon row of back-to-back terraced housing once stood. We played football, cricket and other games there, while relationships were strengthened and romance sometimes blossomed. Most of us children could not recall the names of the streets that stood where we played, and I don't think any of us ever considered why that part of Liverpool, near the docks, was so deeply scarred. But older folks remembered. They recalled the nights of terror, when the bombs were dropping and they prayed to see morning. Unlike them, we knew of nothing different. Our neighbourhood always looked this way. We were used to it and never expected anything to change.

Then the fun began in earnest some 25 years after the end of the war. It had been decided to rebuild and redevelop the area; 'urban regeneration', we were told. The project was long, costly and devastating to those who remembered and liked things the way they always had been, at least for a generation. Rebuilding a devastated city has its problems, whether in post-war Liverpool or fifth-century BC Jerusalem, as the book of Nehemiah graphically illustrates.

Why Nehemiah? Because it is so easy to become dispirited in the work of God, especially in places that once seemed so full of spiritual life and are now littered with disused, renovated or demolished churches and chapels. The toll of the years saps the idealism of youth and vision is lost. The days are difficult, the work is endless, the labourers are few and the resources limited. Many servants of God are tired *in* if not *of* the work. What a tonic Nehemiah is for everyone who is 'weary in doing good' (Galatians 6:9). Welcome to 'Rebuilding a Ruin'.

....

Praying

The words of Nehemiah son of Hakaliah:

In the month of Kislev in the twentieth year, while I was in the citadel of Susa, Hanani, one of my brothers, came from Judah with some other men, and I questioned them about the Jewish remnant that had survived the exile, and also about Jerusalem.

They said to me, 'Those who survived the exile and are back in the province are in great trouble and disgrace. The wall of Jerusalem is broken down, and its gates have been burned with fire.'

When I heard these things, I sat down and wept. For some days I mourned and fasted and prayed before the God of heaven. Then I said:

'Lord, the God of heaven, the great and awesome God, who keeps his covenant of love with those who love him and keep his commandments, let your ear be attentive and your eyes open to hear the prayer your servant is praying before you day and night for your servants, the people of Israel.'

NEHEMIAH 1:1–6A

How wise the old Puritan who said, 'When God intends great mercy for his people, he sets them a-praying.' Nehemiah became part of an amazing movement for change, calling into play all his skills as a visionary leader, motivator, fundraiser, diplomat and all-round action man. But most of all he was a man of prayer. And, as someone has remarked, what we are in prayer is what we are, no more, no less.

First, however, some historical background might help. Traditional dating locates Nehemiah's return to Jerusalem in 445BC, just over 140 years since the sacking of Jerusalem in 587–586BC and the deportation of its citizens, the exile to Babylon. A return took place in 538BC under Joshua and Zerubbabel, amid much optimism (Ezra 1—3). Sadly, the momentum quickly dissipated, and it took the preaching of Haggai and Zechariah in 520BC to rekindle enthusiasm for the rebuilding of the temple. Again, time passed until the return of Ezra in 458BC. According to Ezra 4:6–23, an attempt was made to rebuild Jerusalem, perhaps around 450BC. However, local opposition and Persian decree soon brought the work to a halt. The scene is thus set for the events recorded in the first chapter of Nehemiah.

I don't know if you have discovered that it can be dangerous to ask questions. Nehemiah's enquiry (v. 2) led him to a whole pile of trouble – and his life's work. The rest of the chapter illustrates how, to use an old-fashioned word, God creates a 'burden' in Nehemiah's heart for Jerusalem. Nehemiah is appalled to learn that its walls are broken down and its gates burned with fire (v. 3). When we are faced by huge tasks and overwhelming odds, we may be driven either to despair or to prayer, or both. In Nehemiah's case, it was prayer, one of the great prayers recorded in the Old Testament. We can isolate several components.

- *Worship* – Sometimes the very worst thing we can do with a problem is to start with it. Nehemiah starts with the Lord, 'the great and awesome God', who keeps his promises, 'his covenant of love' (v. 5). Such worship is no chore but a delight (v. 11). A guide at Westminster Abbey was once asked where he worshipped. 'Oh, I am so busy showing folk around the Abbey,' he replied, 'that I never get to a place of worship myself.' Busyness in God's work is never a substitute for getting to a place of worship ourselves.
- *Intensity* – Twice Nehemiah asks for God's ear to be attentive (vv. 6, 11). Three times the King James Version adds 'I beseech' (vv. 5, 8, 11), a translation of a small Hebrew word used by a person

seeking to beg a favour from someone able to answer the request. It is the sense of pleading, realising only God can help. Sometimes our prayers fail here. If God does not show up – well, we must find some other way!

- *Confession* – Though comparatively brief, Nehemiah's prayer is panoramic. National, ancestral and personal sins of omission ('we have not obeyed') and commission ('we have acted very wickedly') are owned and confessed (vv. 6–7). Genuine confession is not only about coming clean with God but also intending to amend our ways (Proverbs 28:13).

- *Request* – This is the element that causes most of the philosophical difficulties about prayer. There is a growth industry in spirituality that is strong on meditation and weak on supplication. However, petitionary prayer is at the heart of biblical praying. And how biblical this petition is! It reverberates with scripture (Leviticus 26:33; Deuteronomy 7:9, 21; 9:29; 30:4). To know the general *will* of God, we need regularly to consult the *word* of God. There are things we never need to ask for in prayer, since God already says they are wrong, and there are promises to claim repeatedly, because they are always right. Nehemiah addresses his requests to the redeemer God who brings people into relationship with himself – '*your* servants' (v. 10, my emphasis).

- *Patience* – 'Day and night' does not indicate that Nehemiah was praying 24/7. Rather, in the apostolic spirit of 'pray continually' (1 Thessalonians 5:17), his morning and evening prayers were focused on one great objective, the welfare of Jerusalem. This focus was sustained for some four months, from the month of Kislev (v. 1) to the month of Nisan (2:1). Delays are not necessarily denials.

- *Sacrifice* – Sometimes our praying stops at the merely devotional. We feel better. There's nothing wrong with that, of course (Psalm 55:22; 1 Peter 5:7). Nehemiah went further. He 'mourned and fasted' (v. 4). The only obligatory fast for Israel was the Day of Atonement ('deny yourselves', Leviticus 16:29), though others were observed (Zechariah 8:19). Too busy to pray? Ever thought of skipping a meal to do so?

- *Faith* – Without faith, a reliance on God and his promises, it is impossible to please him (Hebrews 11:6). Faith puts the world in focus. So, in Nehemiah's prayer, the most powerful man of the day, Artaxerxes, is only 'this man' (v. 11). Nehemiah asks to be given success before the king. Since royal policy had recently stopped Jerusalem's rebuilding (Ezra 4:21), this was a big ask. There are times when faith must be spelt r-i-s-k. Such a time had arrived.
- *Availability* – I can almost imagine Nehemiah's prayers along these lines: 'Lord, that work needs a man of vision and drive. They are like a ship without a rudder.' *Pray on, Nehemiah!* 'Lord, they need someone to approach the king and alter royal policy.' *That's correct, Nehemiah.* 'Lord, please prepare and raise him up soon.' *I have, Nehemiah.* 'Who?' *You!* 'Who? Me?' *Yes, you!* Nehemiah quite simply was willing to be the answer to his prayer. Sometimes the person who gets the vision gets the job. Could it be our prayers have not been answered because we are unwilling to be at least part of the answer?

Monday

....

Influencing

In the month of Nisan in the twentieth year of King Artaxerxes, when wine was brought for him, I took the wine and gave it to the king. I had not been sad in his presence before, so the king asked me, 'Why does your face look so sad when you are not ill? This can be nothing but sadness of heart.'

I was very much afraid, but I said to the king, 'May the king live forever! Why should my face not look sad when the city where my ancestors are buried lies in ruins, and its gates have been destroyed by fire?'

The king said to me, 'What is it you want?'

Then I prayed to the God of heaven, and I answered the king, 'If it pleases the king and if your servant has found favour in his sight, let him send me to the city in Judah where my ancestors are buried so that I can rebuild it.'

And because the gracious hand of my God was on me, the king granted my requests.

NEHEMIAH 2:1–5, 8

A seemingly insignificant sentence knits together the first and second chapters of Nehemiah, 'I was cupbearer to the king' (1:11). Many of us feel powerless to change situations around us. We are not well-connected or particularly clever. But we are concerned for the welfare of our particular 'Jerusalem'. We do well to pray. Some Christians, however, do find themselves by birth, gift or sheer effort, or a combination of all three, in positions of authority and influence. Nehemiah was such a man. He was the king's cupbearer, a position of great trust, since the king's life depended upon him.

It is always encouraging to know that when God calls us to a task, he doesn't leave us without the benefit of preparation. Cupbearing may seem a far cry from wall-building, but the distance is not nearly so great as may initially be imagined. After all, Nehemiah had hardly walked into Artaxerxes' palace one day and simply applied for the post of cupbearer. The untold story of Nehemiah's rise to high office can only be imagined. Whatever his humble immigrant beginning may have been, it was perhaps, as with Daniel and his friends (Daniel 1), supplemented by a thorough education. Then a fast-track entry as a first-class graduate to the Persian civil service, plus hard work, loyalty and service, had paid dividends. He had clearly been faithful in little. He had been well trained in much. He now had a great deal to offer his king – and his God.

Many people feel tremendously hampered by their background. Some, of course, are born with a silver spoon in their mouths. But if the spoon was a substitute for parental love and closeness, they may battle with an inability to be in touch with their emotions well into their mature years. Others are born in poverty, graduate from the college of hard knocks and carry chips on their shoulders for their poor start in life. Nehemiah is an encouragement to all. His name means 'whom the Lord has comforted'. After all, if 'redemption' (1:10) means anything, it entails redeeming all of who we are. It finds us as we are with our backgrounds, idiosyncrasies, prejudices and foibles. To leave us there? It's my observation as a Christian minister that those who master the art of successful Christian living have stopped making their background the foreground of their lives. If I am a Christian, I am a child of God, called to be different, since in and because of Jesus I am different. Where I am headed is more important than where I've come from – that's comfort indeed.

Nehemiah's position, of course, was not fortuitous. He was the right man in the right place at the right time to do the right thing for one simple reason: 'because the gracious hand of my God was on me' (v. 8). Although the book bears his name, it ultimately is not about him. It is about the Lord and his ways with humanity. When God has a piece of work that needs to be done, those he calls to do it will inevitably find that he has been preparing them in all sorts of ways for the task ahead.

At some point in our lives, it is possible to conclude, because of age, location and lack of talent and education, that, unlike Nehemiah, we will never be people of real influence. Really? Edmond Locard (1877–1966) was a forensic scientist who formulated one of its basic principles: 'Every contact leaves a trace.' That is why crime scenes are sealed off as soon as possible to discover any evidence, DNA samples being one of the more recent types. We are all influencers! Some of us will recall singing songs like 'Jesus bids us shine with a clear pure light… you in your small corner and I in mine.' You are a person of influence. Leave a trace for Jesus today.

Tuesday

Organising

By night I went out through the Valley Gate towards the Jackal Well and the Dung Gate, examining the walls of Jerusalem, which had been broken down, and its gates, which had been destroyed by fire. Then I moved on towards the Fountain Gate and the King's Pool, but there was not enough room for my mount to get through; so I went up the valley by night, examining the wall. Finally, I turned back and re-entered through the Valley Gate. The officials did not know where I had gone or what I was doing, because as yet I had said nothing to the Jews or the priests or nobles or officials or any others who would be doing the work.

Then I said to them, 'You see the trouble we are in: Jerusalem lies in ruins, and its gates have been burned with fire. Come, let us rebuild the wall of Jerusalem, and we will no longer be in disgrace.' I also told them about the gracious hand of my God on me and what the king had said to me.

They replied, 'Let us start rebuilding.' So they began this good work.

NEHEMIAH 2:13–18

The internal combustion engine has revolutionised the world. Many of us, however, take it for granted as we turn the ignition key and our car engine fires into life. What then? On many vehicles, we depress the clutch, engage the gear, increase the acceleration and away we go. Have you ever stopped to consider how all that power generated in the engine turns your car's wheels? Simple, really! A network of mechanical and electrical relationships called 'the transmission' does it all for us.

Prayer is God's internal combustion engine. It generates tremendous power that is intended, through a network of relationships, to turn the wheels of progress for the kingdom of God. The second and third chapters of Nehemiah give an insight into the spiritual transmission that converts prayer into action. We concentrate on several elements.

Nehemiah's position as cupbearer meant he was the right person in the right place, as we have noted. Some years ago, a missionary friend wrote in his newsletter of the gap-year student working alongside him. The student, my friend said, had many fine qualities and a desire to serve the Lord, but there was a sticking point: 'As yet he must learn to fit in, and work cheerfully in the inconspicuous.' Whether Nehemiah was a fast-track graduate or received his initial training washing dishes in the royal kitchens, we don't know. However, the old maxim still holds: 'Bloom where you are planted.' 'To work cheerfully in the inconspicuous': do we? If not, may that be the reason why God can't trust us with a more significant role? We need to remember that nothing is inconspicuous or insignificant if it is done out of love for the Lord – whether it be cups of wine for a king or cold water for a disciple (Mark 9:41).

The unfolding events in the rest of chapters 2 and 3 could be entitled 'How to win friends and influence people'[12] as Nehemiah procures royal assent for his expeditionary force to rebuild Jerusalem. Having acquainted himself with the size of the task and having appealed to the people for help (vv. 13–18), he organises the troops. Lots of different skills are needed for rebuilding a city, but the availability of people is paramount. Our Lord reminds us that when it comes to building the city of God through the proclamation of the gospel, so often 'the harvest is plentiful, but the workers are few' (Luke 10:2). Amazingly, Nehemiah takes on the mammoth task of rebuilding the city walls without today's heavy earth-moving equipment and a paid workforce. How did he manage to accomplish it in 52 days (6:15)? Indeed, how do we cope with any overwhelming task? Let Nehemiah help us via his organisational management. Everyone had:

- *A part to play* – organisers, foremen, rubble clearers, hod carriers, etc.
- *An area to work* – some near their homes (3:23) and others who presumably travelled into Jerusalem (3:2, 27).
- *A unity to maintain* – the sheer variety of people involved is fascinating: priests and Levites (3:1, 17), nobles and rulers (3:5, 19), gifted goldsmiths and delicate-handed perfumers, alongside merchants (3:8, 32), women along with men (3:12).
- *A truth to believe* – we cannot leave chapter 3 without wondering why God should deem it important that 32 verses of scripture be devoted to recording what is seemingly a list of employees on an ancient building site. Is it just for the record? Yes, God's record! Ever felt overlooked? No one's said, 'thank you'? Thinking, 'Well, I won't do that again'? Then take a deep draught of this: 'God is not unjust; he will not forget your work and the love you have shown him as you have helped his people and continue to help them' (Hebrews 6:10). The reward for being a 'city of God' builder, ancient or modern, will one day outshine the sun and outlast the stars.

Let's be ready to clear some rubble or lay another stone today.

Wednesday

....

Coping

Meanwhile, the people in Judah said, 'The strength of the labourers is giving out, and there is so much rubble that we cannot rebuild the wall.'
NEHEMIAH 4:10

A man went to his doctor complaining that, as he dropped off to sleep each night, a song about 'the green, green grass of home' would start playing on his mind. Seeking peace, he'd turn over, only to hear another reverberating in his head about a woman named Delilah, whom he said he never knew. Seeking to help him, the doctor assured him that he had Tom Jones syndrome, as the two songs in question were two of the greatest hits of the world-renowned Welsh singer. The patient enquired whether his condition was rare. At that point the doctor started singing, 'It's not unusual.' Pressure, burn out, wanting to give up, downing tools and walking away – is that a rare condition? It's not unusual! The question is how do we address it?

At one level, pressure is inevitable for a Christian. Although the Saviour offers rest for our souls (Matthew 11:29) and a peace that transcends understanding (Philippians 4:7), the fact that we are Christians in a hostile world will inevitably produce strains. In UK society, as secularism bites, there are an increasing number of no-go areas for consistent faith. At work, can you tell a white lie to cover for the boss or turn a blind eye to bullying, racism and sexism? If you are single, is it okay to engage in sex outside marriage, since 'everybody does'? If married, am I supposed to stay with a person whom I no longer feel I love? Illustrations could be multiplied. In this section, we are, however, particularly directed to the real pressures that arise in doing God's work on the front line. Let's consider some symptoms and solutions to potential burnout.

Symptoms of pressure

Three symptoms are highlighted here: strength fails; rubbish increases; work grinds to a halt. Take the first, *strength fails*. That's understandable. Many of the workers were not built for hard labour, as chapter 3 illustrates. However, there are times when the fittest and strongest may feel they can't cope. We can become physically, mentally and spiritually drained, and tempted to think of ourselves as utter failures. Is that your problem in that pastorate, youth fellowship, ladies' Bible study group? But why were they so weary? Because *rubbish increases*. The sheer enormity of the task must have seemed overwhelming: some 140 years of accumulated rubble to move, a massive workforce to organise, new foundations to lay in several areas, and then the wall rebuilding could commence in earnest! I recall years ago leaving my revision for exams late. Suddenly, I felt paralysed by how much there was to do. Like these folks, my work was about to *grind to a halt*: 'we cannot rebuild the wall'.

Solutions to pressure

Are we to carry on regardless? Or sink into inactivity, self-pity and despair? The rest of the chapter illustrates several wise strategies for coping with pressure: our part; others' part; God's part.

- *Remember the Lord – our part* (v. 14): Often here's the essence of our problem – we forget the Lord! The word Nehemiah used means to think on, imprint on your mind, actively recall, the Lord. Haven't we all noticed how near impossible it is to concentrate fully on two things at the same time? So, when we are under pressure, we are called to 'set our minds on things above', 'consider him [Jesus]' and be 'transformed by the renewing of our minds', learning to 'think about such things' (Colossians 3:2; Hebrews 12:3; Romans 12:2; Philippians 4:8). Nehemiah reminds the people of the greatness, power and majesty of their God. The late, great G. Campbell Morgan reportedly said in one of his many sermons: 'The whole difference between faith and fear is that of putting our "buts" before or after "God": God commands, but there are difficulties – that is *paralysis*! There are difficulties, but God commands – *that is power*!' When we remember the Lord, we put the 'but' in the right place.

- *Share the load – others' part* (v. 16): These leaders were posted in positions of vulnerability to assess, protect, defend and encourage their fellow-labourers. One of the great temptations when under pressure is to feel alone. It is in such times that we should be especially thankful for 'the fellowship of the saints'. Our Lord Jesus had three others with him in the garden of Gethsemane to watch and pray. Thank God when he sends us a godly pastor, or wise and sensitive Christian, to pray with us and help 'carry each other's burdens' (Galatians 6:2). Don't despise or shun such 'angels unawares'.

- *Our God will fight for us – his part* (v. 20): This is not merely positive thinking. Beyond such human help, Nehemiah brings us face-to-face with the uncontrollable: the true and living God who acts. He fights for his people, and defends, guards and intervenes on our behalf.

Under pressure? It's not unusual. Remember the Lord. Share the load. Your God will fight for you!

Thursday

....

Rectifying

Now the men and their wives raised a great outcry against their fellow Jews. Some were saying, 'We and our sons and daughters are numerous; in order for us to eat and stay alive, we must get grain.'

Others were saying, 'We are mortgaging our fields, our vineyards and our homes to get grain during the famine.'

Still others were saying, 'We have had to borrow money to pay the king's tax on our fields and vineyards. Although we are of the same flesh and blood as our fellow Jews and though our children are as good as theirs, yet we have to subject our sons and daughters to slavery. Some of our daughters have already been enslaved, but we are powerless, because our fields and our vineyards belong to others.'

When I heard their outcry and these charges, I was very angry. I pondered them in my mind and then accused the nobles and officials. I told them, 'You are charging your own people interest!' So I called together a large meeting to deal with them and said: 'As far as possible, we have bought back our fellow Jews who were sold to the Gentiles. Now you are selling your own people, only for them to be sold back to us!' They kept quiet, because they could find nothing to say.

NEHEMIAH 5:1–8

It seems that hardly a day goes by without the media reporting some further scandal in a church or denomination: misappropriation of funds; a sexual misdemeanour; a leader denying central doctrines of the faith. Here we are reminded that abuse within the believing community is sadly not a new phenomenon.

One word sums up the feelings expressed in the opening verses by the landless, mortgaged-up-to-the-hilt and exorbitantly taxed classes – injustice. As it inevitably does, injustice was breeding profound resentment. In a politically volatile situation like Jerusalem, that would be bad enough. What if the resentment also bred insurrection and boiled over into full-scale revolution? However, for Nehemiah, there was something closer to home. Jewish nobles and officials, not some outsiders, were responsible for the financial exploitation being perpetrated (v. 7). That stung.

The blind spots of fellow believers are often painful indeed. We so easily mistake the impartation of spiritual *life* that new birth brings for the possession of advanced spiritual *sight*. They are not synonyms. The pages of the New Testament are replete with calls to grow up in our faith, to become mature, to train ourselves 'to distinguish good from evil' (Hebrews 5:14). New believers need not only the Spirit's grace and vitality; they equally need the scripture's teaching and training. The apostle, who commands believers to 'be filled with the Spirit' (Ephesians 5:18), equally lays on them precise ethical demands for discipleship, such as, 'Anyone who has been stealing must steal no longer' (4:28). The Spirit and the word are like the two oars in a rowing boat. You need to utilise both to make headway.

The root of the problem Nehemiah faced is familiar enough. As the sage put it, 'When someone tells you it is the principle of the thing, not the money, you can be certain of one thing: it's the money!' Perhaps that is why scripture has so much to say about the wise use of money, on the one hand, and, on the other, its hideous power to blind our hearts to compassion and bind our souls to its destructive force. The love of it is still a root of all kinds of evil (1 Timothy 6:10). And all kinds of evil are in evidence in Nehemiah's community, slave-trading included (vv. 5, 8). So, what is to be done?

Thankfully, Nehemiah is not one of those peace-at-any-price-and-turn-a-blind-eye types. It might have been political suicide to ignore such injustice because of the resentment it bred. For Nehemiah, however, it is much more personal and spiritual. These people have forgotten 'the fear of God' (v. 9). So he is very angry, though wisely he takes time to think before acting (vv. 6–7). A wholesale racket was being conducted. Sometimes personal rebuke is enough. But when sin is in the public domain, a public meeting and reprimand is necessary. The perpetrators are shamed into silence (v. 8), and a promise of compensation for financial irregularities and a commitment not to repeat their practices is extracted (v. 12). Nehemiah recognises the deceitfulness of the heart, especially where money is concerned, so he ensures the promises made are legally binding (v. 12). No wonder there was a fervent 'Amen' and praise offered to God (v. 13). Presumably, those who had been sinned against also willingly forgave. Sad to say some believers nurse grudges for years that gnaw at the soul and grieve the Spirit, long after those who have hurt them have sought forgiveness and made restitution. Such is a million miles away from 'forgiving each other, just as in Christ God forgave you' (Ephesians 4:32).

Perhaps I may add a 'health warning' about dealing with wrongdoing in our own backyards. The rest of the chapter (vv. 14–19) speaks of Nehemiah's personal integrity, which is in stark contrast to others around him. The root of his personal integrity was his 'reverence for God' (v. 15). When we are dealing with messed-up people and situations, we cannot excuse ourselves from the task by claiming that 'no one is perfect'. On the other hand, we must be people of integrity in thought, word and deed. When we are, we will not be afraid to pray with Nehemiah, 'Remember me with favour, my God' (v. 19). He will.

Friday

....

Completing

He had been hired to intimidate me so that I would commit a sin by doing this, and then they would give me a bad name to discredit me. Remember Tobiah and Sanballat, my God, because of what they have done; remember also the prophet Noadiah and how she and the rest of the prophets have been trying to intimidate me. So the wall was completed on the twenty-fifth of Elul, in fifty-two days.

NEHEMIAH 6:13–15

We had engaged him in good faith. The quality of his work was commendable. Three years on, however, and amid promises galore, the tradesman still had not delivered. In management-speak, whatever else he was, a completer-finisher he was not. Although every Christian is, by the grace of God, a work in progress, in the Lord's service there are far more starters than finishers. Sadly, too many churches and institutions are illustrations of half-finished towers (Luke 14:28–30). Nehemiah had no intention of that being his epitaph. However, dark forces might well have done. One of the principles of spiritual warfare is illustrated in this chapter: 'Strike the shepherd, and the sheep will be scattered' (Zechariah 13:7; Matthew 26:31). It should therefore not surprise us, if we are leaders, to discover that we are prime targets of the enemy. That's why we need to put on 'the full armour of God' (Ephesians 6:11). Let Nehemiah help to show us how.

Don't get sidetracked

The invitation for a pow-wow with his enemies in a village some 20 miles from Jerusalem was subtle. It might have contained a touch of flattery: 'You are really important, Nehemiah, we need you at this meeting!' Some of us are diverted from our primary calling by the temptation to be seen in the right company and viewed as a rising star. We can mortgage today and sacrifice tomorrow. Nehemiah, however, was clear on his priorities: 'I am carrying on a great project and cannot go down' (v. 3). The tyranny of the urgent in his case was justified, to finish the job. Happy the leader who knows what God has created them for and called them to. Which is my particular wall? Does my schedule and diary reflect that?

Don't be too sensitive

Having declined the train ride of distraction, Nehemiah now faces a roller coaster ride of personal intimidation. The tabloid press of the day – 'an unsealed letter' (v. 5) – means everyone can read it. Jerusalem's politically volatile past would add credibility to the allegation that Nehemiah had had himself proclaimed king and was leading a revolt (vv. 6–7). Innuendo has ruined many good men and women. But Nehemiah's response is brilliant: a curt 'you are just making it up out of your head' (v. 8). He quickly recognises the enemy's tactic is to make them 'too weak for the work' (v. 9). The opposition backfired, and fortified Nehemiah to finish the job.

But Nehemiah is still not out of the woods. Enter the 'word from God' brigade, Shemaiah.

Don't become too spiritual

The phrase 'shut in at his home' (v. 10) may suggest either a state of prophetic ecstasy or an acted parable for Nehemiah's imminent danger: Nehemiah needed to be shut in the temple. Why is this a problem? If we accept the possibility of a direct word from God today, then the tests referred to in this passage are crucial. First, there is scripture itself. Numbers 18:7 clearly forbade, on pain of death, the kind of going into the temple that Shemaiah implies. Second, the message itself did not have the right feel. It clearly peddled the kind of soft option to which Jeremiah alludes in speaking of false prophets: 'They speak visions from their own minds... "you will have peace... No harm will come to you"' (Jeremiah 23:16–17). Third, the fruit of such a message needs to be assessed. Nehemiah clearly saw such a course as demeaning ('Should a man like me run away?') and leading into sin (vv. 11, 13). Finally, the character of the 'prophet' needs to be checked: Shemaiah was a charlatan who prophesied for money (v. 12).

'So the wall was completed' on 15 September, some 2,460 years ago (v. 15). Josephus tells us that it took two years and four months.[13] That would include all the necessary finishing touches. Nehemiah's vision had been amply fulfilled. He had prayed, planned, parried and stood firm. His enemies conceded that the work had been accomplished with the help of God, were afraid and lost confidence (v. 16).

Was Nehemiah, then, all finished? Unfortunately, God's enemies seem to have the optimism of the average football supporter: 'Defeat? What defeat? There's always next season!' The loss of self-confidence was only temporary, for the chapter (and the book itself) ends with Nehemiah still facing problems: 'And Tobiah sent letters to intimidate me' (v. 19). Eternal vigilance continues to be the price of freedom. There will always be battles to face, mountains to climb, valleys to conquer. God has promised to wipe away every tear from our eyes – one day (Revelation 21:4). Meanwhile, Nehemiah remained just as dependent on God when the walls were up as he was before. There are broken walls in marriages, homes, churches, communities and the world. They all need God's help and a Nehemiah-like tenacity to see the job through to completion.

The year 2017 marked the hundredth anniversary of the USA's entry into World War I. George M. Cohan's patriotic hit song 'Over There' assured the Allies, 'The Yanks are coming' to Europe. But for how long? The promise of the song was: 'We won't come back till it's over, over there!' Nehemiah, the consummate completer-finisher, likewise went nowhere till the job was done. God grant us such tenacity in our 'Jerusalem' today.

Saturday

....

Reforming

One of the sons of Joiada son of Eliashib the high priest was son-in-law to Sanballat the Horonite. And I drove him away from me.

Remember them, my God, because they defiled the priestly office and the covenant of the priesthood and of the Levites.

So I purified the priests and the Levites of everything foreign, and assigned them duties, each to his own task. I also made provision for contributions of wood at designated times, and for the firstfruits.

Remember me with favour, my God.

NEHEMIAH 13:28–31

At a leaders' conference many years ago, one of the speakers, while encouraging churches to purchase resources to help their minister, humorously remarked: 'It's always easier to raise £100,000 to fix the leak in the roof of the church than to raise £10,000 to help the drip in the pulpit!' The unvarnished truth is that it is far easier to put up structures and rebuild a city, Nehemiah-like, than to change people.

Chapters 7—13 of Nehemiah deserve at least a skim read, so we can put together the flow of the book. There has been a phase for *rebuilding the walls* (chs 1—6). Now it's high time for *reviving the people* (7—10) and *re-establishing the city* (11—13).

Reviving the people (chs 7—10)

It has been well said that if we do not know where we have come from we may not know where we're going. The genealogy in chapter 7 reminds this motley and disparate crew that they are part of God's purposes in history. That identity is underlined when Ezra reads and explains the scriptures to them, from a 'high wooden platform' (8:4) – the only place in the Bible where a pulpit is mentioned! Was this dull, boring preaching? Hardly, for the word of God moved them to tears (8:9). Does that happen in your church or personal life? The tears were a staging post, not a destination, the precursor to discovering their strength in 'the joy of the Lord' (8:10). There was also the need for confession of sin and for forgiveness, as is graphically illustrated in chapter 9 (it is worth highlighting the pronouns of the chapter: 'you' – what God does in grace; 'they' – what they did in sin).

I recently watched a YouTube clip of Donald Trump before his election as president. The interviewer asked him about whether he had ever asked God for forgiveness. His initial answer spoke very warmly about his church and his favourite preacher, Dr Norman Vincent Peale (1898–1993), the world-famous author of *The Power of Positive Thinking*. The interviewer, however, pressed him about asking for forgiveness. Mr Trump continued to prevaricate, adding that when he did wrong he tried to do better next time.

That may appear to be an admirable trait – learn from your mistakes and do better next time – but it ultimately denies what is essential to Christian faith. Reportedly, C.S. Lewis, when on a radio panel, was asked, 'What can Jesus Christ give me that no one else can, and I'd like the answer in one word?' His reply was immediate: 'Forgiveness!' Based on such forgiveness, the people enter a covenant with God, a binding spiritual commitment not to 'neglect the house of our God' (10:39). Always a great idea.

Re-establishing the city (chs 11—13)

There are three ingredients in these three chapters that we neglect at our peril if we are to hope to impact our communities and the great metropolises of the world for the gospel: incarnation (ch. 11); celebration (ch. 12); reformation (ch. 13).

When people are drowning out at sea, lifeboats tucked up safely in harbour rescue no one. Nehemiah knew his city needed more than gates and walls for its rescue. It needed people prepared to move into Jerusalem – *incarnation* (ch. 11). When the Lord came to save his lost world, he changed addresses: 'The Word became flesh and made his dwelling among us' (John 1:14). Likewise, Christians moving into a city need to be a 'God-send'.

However, if they don't come with the previously mentioned 'joy of the Lord' (8:10), then the city already has enough of its own misery to be going on with. Accordingly, chapter 12 illustrates a great *celebration*, for the Lord is worthy, and its celebrants are called to be an attractive, worshipping community.

As Nehemiah's narrative closes, we might be tempted to say, along with the now famous Kenneth Wolstenholme quote from the 1966 FIFA World Cup final, 'they think it's all over'. Not quite! For in the final four verses Nehemiah prays two things: about ongoing failure in the community – 'Remember them, my God, because they defiled the priestly office' (v. 29); and a personal request – 'Remember me with favour, my God' (v. 31). The work of *reformation* must continue through rebuilding, reviving and re-establishing the work of God. Do you think it's all over where you live and work and serve the Lord? Of course not. But one day we will hear the Lord's version of the rest of Wolstenholme's quote: 'It is now!' Then the endless celebrations will begin in earnest.

Week 4

Creating communities of faith: unpredictable churches

As we approach a week of readings from the book of Revelation, we are introduced to seven first-century churches that speak powerfully to the churches of both their day and ours. Note the repeated phrase after every letter, 'what the Spirit says/is saying to the churches'. Some commentators have seen successive 'church ages' being forecast here – and they often conclude we are in the last phase, the church's Laodicean period. However, the more immediate application is that here is not so much an *ideal* church or forecast of history but the *real* church as it finds her place in the world and in God's redemptive flow of history until the Lord returns. When he does, the church will be 'as a bride beautifully dressed for her husband' – indeed, the very epitome of all the hopes and aspirations of what the new Jerusalem entails and will be (Revelation 21:1—22:6).

If we learn little else from these churches, two lessons should keep us going. First, there is no one 'silver bullet' for the ills of the church. These different churches needed different solutions. Imagine a doctor prescribing the same treatment, aspirin for example, for every presenting symptom, ranging from mild headaches to life-threatening cancers. Likewise, beware of ecclesiastical panaceas. Second, beware of blanket condemnations of the type, 'The church is always, never, should be, etc.' For a bit of fun, try changing the address on each of these seven churches. For example, Laodicea is commended but Smyrna is rebuked for being lukewarm.

Welcome to the church as it is, and churches as they are in the world, then and now, and on their way to the new Jerusalem.

Sunday

....

Sound Street Abbey – Ephesus

'To the angel of the church in Ephesus write:

These are the words of him who holds the seven stars in his right hand and walks among the seven golden lampstands. I know your deeds, your hard work and your perseverance. I know that you cannot tolerate wicked people, that you have tested those who claim to be apostles but are not, and have found them false. You have persevered and have endured hardships for my name, and have not grown weary.

Yet I hold this against you: You have forsaken the love you had at first. Consider how far you have fallen! Repent and do the things you did at first. If you do not repent, I will come to you and remove your lampstand from its place. But you have this in your favour: you hate the practices of the Nicolaitans, which I also hate.

Whoever has ears, let them hear what the Spirit says to the churches. To the one who is victorious, I will give the right to eat from the tree of life, which is in the paradise of God.'

REVELATION 2:1–7

In her now famous interview with Martin Bashir, when asked whether she would ever be queen, the much-lamented Diana, Princess of Wales, memorably remarked, 'I'd like to be a queen of people's hearts.' The church at Ephesus must have felt shocked when they heard something similar from Jesus, as he was not king of theirs.

Founded by the apostle Paul nearly 40 years previously, this church had become a centre of evangelistic outreach in a renowned commercial centre. Its awesome temple to Artemis (Diana) was one of the seven wonders of the ancient world. In this city, the gospel had progressed remarkably well (Acts 19:1–20). The church was also the proud possessor of a magnificent epistle, Ephesians, full of sound doctrine and prescriptions for practical Christian living. Accordingly, years later, it was still a hard-working, biblically sound church, able quickly to sniff and snuff out heresy (vv. 2, 3, 6). In over 40 years of ordained ministry, it has been my privilege to have served four churches as pastor where such commitments to the Lord and his word have been their hallmark. In them, preaching and teaching the scriptures were given priority in worship services. Not there the five-minute sermonette, for the conviction was that sermonettes make Christianettes. (That said, I have heard some spectacularly good short sermons and some incredibly long, monotonous monologues!) But it's possible to have such things right and still not please the Lord.

One of the get-out clauses of financial advice is 'past performance is no guarantee of future growth'. Sadly, this applied to this Ephesian church. Instead of Jesus being its 'king of hearts', it had lost its first love (v. 4). They were still going through the motions, working hard, hanging on in there, doing the business, staying orthodox (v. 2). But the passion had gone. At Moorlands College, our mission statement says we exist 'to train people *passionate* about Jesus Christ'. In every sphere of life we recognise passion, and know when it's missing: the teacher and her student; the football coach and his player; the boss and their clock-watching employee; the wife and her husband of many years. In *Fiddler on the Roof*, Tevye repeatedly asks Golde, his sharp-tongued wife, a question that is the title of the song: 'Do you love me?' She reels off all the things she does for him. 'But do you love me?' he continues to ask. Similarly, like many churches and individuals, the Ephesians had forgotten that loving the Lord with all our heart and soul is not a sideshow in the Christian life but the main event – to love him 'with an undying love', as Paul's letter to them had intimated (Ephesians 6:24). So, Jesus calls us in love to consider (or remember) how far we may have fallen, and to do something about it: to repent (v. 5).

Princess Diana could not and did not die for us. Jesus did. Rightly, he is king of hearts. Let's enthrone him afresh today, and serve him with renewed passion, with a first love, as he walks not only among the seven golden lampstands of his churches but the recesses of our hearts today (v. 1). Well may we pray the words of this verse from a hymn by William Cowper (1731–1800):

Lord, it is my chief complaint
That my love is weak and faint.
Yet I love you and adore
Oh, for grace to love you more.

Monday

Crown Close Cathedral – Smyrna

'To the angel of the church in Smyrna write:

These are the words of him who is the First and the Last, who died and came to life again. I know your afflictions and your poverty – yet you are rich! I know about the slander of those who say they are Jews and are not, but are a synagogue of Satan. Do not be afraid of what you are about to suffer. I tell you, the devil will put some of you in prison to test you, and you will suffer persecution for ten days. Be faithful, even to the point of death, and I will give you life as your victor's crown.

Whoever has ears, let them hear what the Spirit says to the churches. The one who is victorious will not be hurt at all by the second death.'

REVELATION 2:8–11

Over its 160-year history, the Victoria Cross (VC) has been awarded only 1,358 times, always for conspicuous bravery, self-sacrifice or extreme devotion to duty in the presence of the enemy. Here another VC is on offer from Jesus himself: 'the victor's crown' (v. 10).

The church in Smyrna certainly had its back to the wall – afflictions, poverty, slander, prison and death awaited some of them. Likewise, when we are going through a tough time, temptations are many and varied on how to quit: capitulate to the enemy; compromise our faith or our morals; even curse God, as Job's wife advised him to do in order to hasten death via a form of spiritual, self-inflicted euthanasia (Job 2:9). Thankfully, the Lord understood all their temptations and trials, and had no criticism for these beleaguered believers. They typify so many believers and churches in many parts of the world today.

Douglas Murray, who describes himself as a Christian atheist, writing recently in *The Spectator*, entitled his article 'Who will protect Nigeria's northern Christians?' Provocatively, the strapline added, 'Every week, there are more massacres, but nobody seems to mind – not even their own government'.[14] The catalogue of rape and murder perpetrated against such believers is unconscionably wicked. 'The Christians of Nigeria are alone,' he adds. 'Even if we don't care about this, we ought to know.' Well, Jesus does know about folk in Smyrna and northern Nigeria (v. 9), and does indeed care for them. Indeed, he cared so much that he died for them, becoming the ultimate martyr (v. 8).

However, God often gets the blame when things go wrong. Except in jest, our secular culture has airbrushed 'Satan', 'the devil', out of our vocabulary (vv. 9–10). Yet here 'our Father below', as C.S. Lewis describes Satan in *The Screwtape Letters*, seems to be very much alive and active. Undoubtedly, there are deep mysteries here. Christians are not cosmic dualists. That is, the Bible's understanding of the 'evil one' is not like the scenarios played out in *Star Wars*, where the Force is neutral and two equal competitors, the light side and the dark side, battle it out. Accordingly, when things look bleak for the church in this final book of the New Testament, it is here we discover the brightest faith. Nine of the ten New Testament references to God being 'Almighty' are found in Revelation (e.g. 19:6). And in this letter Jesus reminds his people that he is 'the First and the Last' (v. 8), echoing both Isaiah 44:6 and repeating Revelation 1:17. In grammar, such a phrase is called a merism, a form of speech where extremities are used ('heaven and earth', 'from east to west', etc.) to refer to everything in between as well. The beginning, the end and everything else – all are under his watchful eye and tender yet all-powerful control and care.

But herein lies the mystery: why and how? If the Lord is so powerful, then how come he allows the devil such opportunity? That is why the future orientation of faith is vital. Like a soccer match, the result is not final till the whistle is blown for full-time. Accordingly, Jesus tells the church in Smyrna to be faithful 'even to the point of death', for their reward awaits – 'the victor's crown' (v. 10). The crown on offer here could be likened to and contrasted with the kind awarded to someone who had done great service in local government or had been victorious at the games, like getting an MBE or winning a medal. Such crowns were also worn at banquets as a mark of festivity, like flowers at a wedding. Inevitably, being made of flowers or weeds, such crowns perished. But the crown Jesus offers is one of life 'that can never perish, spoil or fade' (1 Peter 1:4), and he is more than able to deliver on his promise.

A man once confidently told me that his recently deceased friend had assured him that when he likewise 'passed over to the other side', that friend would be waiting for him. On what basis did he build such faith? Pious optimism, I fear. But Jesus can deliver, because he both died and 'came to life again' (v. 8). Thinking of quitting? Feeling you have had enough? Remember the VC. Like those first-century recipients, be loyal to heaven's government, keep running the race of faith and remember a banquet with the king is being prepared. Well may we pray today, 'Lord, keep my focus on the crown, even when I feel under a cross!'

Tuesday

Martyr's Memorial Church – Pergamum

'To the angel of the church in Pergamum write:

These are the words of him who has the sharp, double-edged sword. I know where you live – where Satan has his throne. Yet you remain true to my name. You did not renounce your faith in me, not even in the days of Antipas, my faithful witness, who was put to death in your city – where Satan lives.

Nevertheless, I have a few things against you: there are some among you who hold to the teaching of Balaam, who taught Balak to entice the Israelites to sin so that they ate food sacrificed to idols and committed sexual immorality. Likewise, you also have those who hold to the teaching of the Nicolaitans. Repent therefore! Otherwise, I will soon come to you and will fight against them with the sword of my mouth.

Whoever has ears, let them hear what the Spirit says to the churches. To the one who is victorious, I will give some of the hidden manna. I will also give that person a white stone with a new name written on it, known only to the one who receives it.'

REVELATION 2:12–17

A few years ago, while on a small Caribbean island, one of my hosts reminded me that things were hard going there for the gospel. Only about two-thirds of the islanders attended church on a Sunday morning, and so many of those churches were 'sound'! I thought a trip to some parts of the north of England would have been reality therapy for him. Although nowhere on earth is a spiritually demilitarised zone, there are some regions that are much tougher for the gospel than others. Pergamum was such a place. It functioned as a centre for emperor worship, the probable meaning of Satan's throne (v. 13). Once a year, citizens were required to show up at a temple, burn incense in Caesar's honour and declare 'Caesar is Lord'. Having done so, and with a written certificate to prove it, they were free to worship any other god or none. Today, religion in its various forms, far from being a dying phenomenon as some atheists had hoped and predicted, is often the glue that brings cohesion to various groups or nations. As the first-century 'Unholy Roman Empire' knew, having all its citizens acknowledge its Caesar as a god, alongside their own religions, would be a cohesive factor in society, a good way of keeping everyone in their place and helping to maintain the Pax Romana, the peace of Rome.

To confess Caesar as Lord, in a world where emperor worship appeared to be the fastest-growing religion, was impossible for Christians, who confessed 'Jesus is Lord'. Conflict was inevitable. Already, Antipas had been martyred for his faithfulness to Christ (v. 13). Indeed, here we note one of those interesting moments when the word 'martyr', meaning 'witness', is beginning to morph into the expanded meaning we think of today: someone laying down their life for their faith. Many other martyrs through history have joined Antipas, right up to the present. Do you know any? It has been my sad privilege to know two. Let me tell you briefly about Mary.

Mary Fisher was a slip of a Welsh girl, with the face and voice of an angel, a fellow student back in the early 1970s at what is now the London School of Theology. She went off to be a teacher in an Elim Pentecostal missionary school in what is now Zimbabwe. In June 1978, she and another dozen missionaries and their children were brutally butchered to death by the so-called Freedom Fighters. A friend, who was an army chaplain at that time, had gone into that carnage. All the birds and animals had fled, nature itself seemingly revolted by such evil. 'You could feel the evil in the air,' he told me. When they found Mary's cassette player, she'd been teaching the children to sing a popular chorus of the time: 'For me to live is Christ, to die is gain'. 'When Christ calls a man,' said Dietrich Bonhoeffer, 'he bids him come and die.'[15] I sometimes look at the students who pass through my college and wonder how many may yet make the ultimate sacrifice for their crucified Lord.

Sometimes, however, as one of the early church fathers, Tertullian, reminds us, 'The blood of the martyrs is the seed of the church.' Persecution and direct opposition may strengthen the church, so we stand more firmly together. When that happens, the devil uses other tactics. The teachings of Balaam and the Nicolaitans appeared to have offered a form of compromise between the world and the church that blurred the lines of demarcation morally and spiritually (for some background, see Numbers 22:1–25:5). Sometimes Satan appears as 'a roaring lion', and at other times 'an angel of light' (1 Peter 5:8; 2 Corinthians 11:14). Whatever his guise, when he is our next-door neighbour (v. 13), we are neither to move house nor invite him round for coffee. Rather, we are to remain faithful to Christ, whose rewards are out of this world: 'hidden manna', 'the bread of angels' (Psalm 78:25), nourishing beyond compare; a 'white stone', often used for casting a vote, so our vote for Christ eternally counts; and a 'new name', so we know we are special indeed (v. 17)!

Wednesday

···

Loose Lane Fellowship – Thyatira

'To the angel of the church in Thyatira write:

These are the words of the Son of God, whose eyes are like blazing fire and whose feet are like burnished bronze. I know your deeds, your love and faith, your service and perseverance, and that you are now doing more than you did at first.

Nevertheless, I have this against you: you tolerate that woman Jezebel, who calls herself a prophet. By her teaching she misleads my servants into sexual immorality and the eating of food sacrificed to idols. I have given her time to repent of her immorality, but she is unwilling. So I will cast her on a bed of suffering, and I will make those who commit adultery with her suffer intensely, unless they repent of her ways. I will strike her children dead. Then all the churches will know that I am he who searches hearts and minds, and I will repay each of you according to your deeds.

Now I say to the rest of you in Thyatira, to you who do not hold to her teaching and have not learned Satan's so-called deep secrets, "I will not impose any other burden on you, except to hold on to what you have until I come."

To the one who is victorious and does my will to the end, I will give authority over the nations – that one "will rule them with an iron sceptre and will dash them to pieces like pottery" – just as I have received authority from my Father. I will also give that one the morning star.

Whoever has ears, let them hear what the Spirit says to
the churches.'
REVELATION 2:18–29

Some time ago, a couple were registering the birth of their son,
Orson. The registrar was mildly inquisitive about his forename
and was told it was because the couple were fans of Orson Welles,
the actor and director. Still expressing some concern, the registrar
pointed out that Orson was fine but, if they added it to their surname,
Cart, it might cause the child some difficulty later. It is not a unique
combination of unfortunate first and final names. However, I suspect
no one would knowingly call their daughter Jezebel, a synonym
for wickedness and debauchery (1 Kings 16—22, 2 Kings 9), unless
they had a long-term death wish! The Jezebel here is probably a
pseudonym for a self-styled prophetess who taught 'deep secrets'
that involved sexual immorality, and were satanically inspired (vv.
20, 24). She did not seek to ravage the church directly. Rather, by
stealth, she sought to change its teachings and practices in a way
that would eventually destroy it. Jezebel has had many successors,
men and women, down the ages.

Ask any church leader for some of the horror stories they have
encountered over the years in this area of sexual misdemeanour.
Indeed, hardly a day passes when some church or denomination
is not in the dock, having to apologise for the misbehaviour of a
philandering priest or an erring member. Of course, such is the wider
social context in which many churches operate and from which
they are not hermetically sealed. Today in the UK, it is not Jezebel
but Jimmy Savile who is a synonym for outrageous sexual abuse,
perpetrated over decades and fuelled by the seeming complicity
of people who should have known better. How many victims might
have been saved from his lechery if someone had intervened in time.

People do mess up. Terrible atrocities are committed all over the
world, by people of different faiths and none. Human nature is not
perfect, to put it mildly. So, what has Christian faith to say to such?

Certainly not what was being offered in Thyatira. There, 'Jezebel insights' and immoral practices were being introduced and tolerated in a Christian community and brought shame to the name of Christ. Clearly, they had forgotten that Christianity professes to be a 'revealed religion' because of a 'faith that was once for all entrusted to God's holy people' (Jude 3). Christian truth, doctrinal and moral, is not a nose of wax to be twisted into the prevailing cultural mores of the day. In Thyatira, Christians were commendably busy (v. 19), as are many church members today. However, they were also turning a blind eye to what was wrong in their fellowship, an attitude that is echoed too often in the contemporary church. Jesus never does; his penetrative gaze misses nothing. His eyes of 'blazing fire' (v. 18) are a reminder both of his omniscience – his X-ray vision we might say – and of his fiery indignation at such compromise. We see things. He sees *through* them to the heart (v. 23).

Are there things being tolerated in your church or personal life that are wounding Christ – false teaching; sexual immorality; financial impropriety; incessant, carping criticism? Despite the seriousness of Jezebel's misdemeanours, it is astonishing that the Lord had allowed her time to change her ways (v. 21). 'With you there is forgiveness,' said the psalmist (130:4). That's the gospel! And it is still the gospel, even when reconciliation with the perpetrator or victim is not possible, and all sorts of painful and temporal consequences have kicked in. However, forgiveness does not rewrite the past of, say, a cheating partner or a sexually abused child. The cross of Christ effects peace *with* God (Romans 5:1), but the damage we have inflicted or suffered might take a long time to, or this side of heaven might never, find a place of peace and reconciliation. That is why it is folly to seek to justify the unjustifiable. God forgives sin not excuses! But such forgiveness is conditional on what Jezebel and her brothel members were unprepared for – a good dose of repentance. They were forgetting that even the patience of God can be exhausted (vv. 22, 23).

Thursday

....

Cemetery Junction Church – Sardis

'To the angel of the church in Sardis write:

These are the words of him who holds the seven spirits of God and the seven stars. I know your deeds; you have a reputation of being alive, but you are dead. Wake up! Strengthen what remains and is about to die, for I have found your deeds unfinished in the sight of my God. Remember, therefore, what you have received and heard; hold it fast, and repent. But if you do not wake up, I will come like a thief, and you will not know at what time I will come to you.

Yet you have a few people in Sardis who have not soiled their clothes. They will walk with me, dressed in white, for they are worthy. The one who is victorious will, like them, be dressed in white. I will never blot out the name of that person from the book of life, but will acknowledge that name before my Father and his angels. Whoever has ears, let them hear what the Spirit says to the churches.'

REVELATION 3:1–6

The company was in great shape. Its reputation, fuelled by its own publicity via its spin doctors, was awesome. But the management consultant had seen it all before: pride spawned by success and deliberate deafness to any warning bells meant it was only a matter of time before the company's 'class act' became a 'crash act'. The trajectory was clear if one had eyes to see and ears to hear. But was anyone looking or listening? When that company is a church and the consultant is Jesus, what folly it is to carry on regardless. Welcome to Sardis, a city built on a rocky plateau and which presented itself as an impregnable fortress. Twice in its history, however, while the city slept, Sardis had been captured. How like its environment the church had become! So Jesus issued a wake-up call (v. 2) to a fellowship that was sleepwalking itself, like any smug business, into liquidation. Their situation highlights a vital principle for Christian engagement with the world.

To paraphrase Dietrich Bonhoeffer: 'Spirituality without worldly involvement ends up in a ghetto, and worldly involvement without a deep spirituality becomes pure boulevard.'[16] On that secular boulevard anything goes. Simultaneously, Christians are called to be 'not *of* the world' but 'sent *into*' it (John 17:14–18), to be salt and light without becoming either bland or invisible (Matthew 5:13–16). Herein lies the challenge for 21st-century churches. I travel widely, especially around the UK. I sometimes visit churches that have become ghettoes. They are certainly not 'of this world' (some might say they are even 'out of it'), and are most certainly not *into* their surrounding neighbourhoods. They may even preen themselves with the thought that they are 'whiter than white' (v. 4). However, being invisible, they make no impact on their world. If their church did not exist on that estate, the question is whether anyone in the locality would notice, especially if most of its members commute to it anyway. On the other hand, some churches are *of* and *into* their communities. They are very busy, and certainly do not appear to be sleeping. But sadly, their members are indistinguishable from the world around them. Anything goes, and the Christian message, driven by a desire for relevance to the prevailing culture, is diluted to the point of irrelevancy. Sardis was such a fellowship, where many, blending into its comparatively wealthy but degenerate city life, had 'soiled their clothes', rather than being 'dressed in white', a sign of both purity and victory (vv. 4, 5).

The Sixth Sense (1999) is a cleverly crafted, Oscar-nominated film in which child psychologist Dr Malcolm Crowe seeks to help a 9-year-old boy, Cole Sear, who is suffering from hallucinations, supposedly seeing ghosts. The twist in the plot is that it turns out that although the good doctor thinks himself alive and well, he is actually dead, and that is the reason Cole can see and talk to him. (I am *not* recommending any of the theology involved here!) Just down the road from where I live is an aptly named location, where you know precisely what does and does not happen there – Cemetery Junction. The problem of the church in Sardis was that they were so close to becoming what the word cemetery originally meant in Greek – a sleeping place or 'dormitory of the dead'.

There is a solution for every church ghetto or boulevard: 'Remember, therefore, what you have received and heard; hold it fast, and repent' (v. 3). And for those of us with unfinished business (v. 2), and who have 'soiled our clothes', we need to come afresh to Jesus, the one who offers cleansing and renewal. Is a trip to the spiritual cleaners overdue for you or your church today? The alternative, if the Lord comes 'like a thief' (v. 3), might, God forbid, be a journey to the cemetery!

Main Road Assembly – Philadelphia

'To the angel of the church in Philadelphia write:

These are the words of him who is holy and true, who holds the key of David. What he opens no one can shut, and what he shuts no one can open. I know your deeds. See, I have placed before you an open door that no one can shut. I know that you have little strength, yet you have kept my word and have not denied my name. I will make those who are of the synagogue of Satan, who claim to be Jews though they are not, but are liars – I will make them come and fall down at your feet and acknowledge that I have loved you. Since you have kept my command to endure patiently, I will also keep you from the hour of trial that is going to come on the whole world to test the inhabitants of the earth.

I am coming soon. Hold on to what you have, so that no one will take your crown. The one who is victorious I will make a pillar in the temple of my God. Never again will they leave it. I will write on them the name of my God and the name of the city of my God, the new Jerusalem, which is coming down out of heaven from my God; and I will also write on them my new name. Whoever has ears, let them hear what the Spirit says to the churches.'

REVELATION 3:7–13

Opportunity Knocks, a forerunner of programmes like *Britain's Got Talent* and *The X Factor*, was an immensely popular British television series in the latter half of last century. It gave unknown performers a platform to showcase their talents and unearthed several stars.

In contrast, the church at Philadelphia was not full of natural superstars. Rather, they were people of 'little strength' (v. 8), unlike their neighbours at no-strength Cemetery Junction Church (v. 1), since they were dead, and max-strength Cool Chapel (v. 17) down the road, who thought themselves to be wonderfully alive. However, this church had enough strength and sense to keep Christ's word and be loyal to his name (vv. 8, 11) and to use what they had, their 'little strength'. Do we?

Elsewhere, Jesus promises that 'whoever has will be given more' and illustrates that principle with a parable about receiving five, two or just one talent (Matthew 25:14–30). The talent indicated in that story was, of course, a unit of money, worth about 20 years of a day-labourer's wage – a huge sum! So, although not the same kind of talents as those on display in *Britain's Got Talent*, it is nevertheless appropriate to view all we have been given – family, location, intellect, musical ability, a caring heart, finances – as gifts on trust to be exercised and utilised for the Master. The tragedy of the man with just one talent in Jesus' story was that he hid it in the ground, bringing utter ruin to himself (Matthew 25:25, 30). The huge lesson, surely, is that regardless of our strength levels, we are actively to employ what we have been given. Even then, danger lurks. Do not despair if you have little strength. On the other hand, when you are blessed with great resources, be like the comedian and actor Lenny Henry. I saw him being interviewed about the period when he began to make it. His dad, who never commented on his career up till then, had a wise piece of advice: 'Don't get too big for your boots!' Indeed 'who makes you different from anyone else? What do you have that you did not receive? And if you did receive it, why do you boast as though you did not?' (1 Corinthians 4:7).

There is an immediate dividend for this church's faithfulness: 'an open door that no one can shut' (v. 8). In other words, there will be greater opportunities beckoning for service to Christ in the community where the Philadelphian church is located. They have not unlocked the door themselves. It is the Lord who opens and shuts (v. 7). Nevertheless, there is a general principle at work here too: 'Whoever can be trusted with very little can also be trusted with much' (Luke 16:10). They used what they had, they did what they could, and the one with all the keys opened further opportunities.

One of the joys of my job at Moorlands is helping to train a whole range of students for Christian service around the globe. However, it is not always the mega-gifted who go far. Occasionally, some of those are waiting for the big break and don't seize the smaller ones to hand. On the other hand, we regularly see averagely gifted students finding doors opening wide for useful gospel ministry. It is so clearly the Lord's doing. They have no pretentions as to their abilities, but they get on with what is in front of them. The secret? They have put the little they have, their 'little strength', at the Lord's disposal. But in the hands of the all-sufficient Christ, little is always much. The truth is simple but profound: when the Lord Jesus is *The X Factor* in our lives, *Opportunity Knocks*.

Saturday

....

Cool Court Chapel – Laodicea

'To the angel of the church in Laodicea write:

These are the words of the Amen, the faithful and true witness, the ruler of God's creation. I know your deeds, that you are neither cold nor hot. I wish you were either one or the other! So, because you are lukewarm – neither hot nor cold – I am about to spit you out of my mouth. You say, "I am rich; I have acquired wealth and do not need a thing." But you do not realise that you are wretched, pitiful, poor, blind and naked. I counsel you to buy from me gold refined in the fire, so that you can become rich; and white clothes to wear, so that you can cover your shameful nakedness; and salve to put on your eyes, so that you can see.

Those whom I love I rebuke and discipline. So be earnest and repent. Here I am! I stand at the door and knock. If anyone hears my voice and opens the door, I will come in and eat with that person, and they with me.

To the one who is victorious, I will give the right to sit with me on my throne, just as I was victorious and sat down with my Father on his throne. Whoever has ears, let them hear what the Spirit says to the churches.'

REVELATION 3:14–22

Holman Hunt's painting *The Light of the World* is one of the earliest memories I have from Sunday school, my first introduction to Christian art. It famously depicts Jesus standing at a door overgrown with weeds, holding his lamp, and knocking for admission. It has often been pointed out that there is no handle on the outside. Here's a door that must be opened from the inside, by people like us. Over the years, this image of Christ knocking at the door of the sinner's heart has been used countless times in public meetings and one-on-one encounters to lead individuals to open their hearts and receive Jesus as Lord and Saviour. For me, it happened some 50 years ago, on 13 March 1967 to be precise, in an evangelistic meeting in our local Anglican church. May I ask if you have likewise opened that door of your heart to Christ?

In its context, however, it is the lamentable situation of the Laodicean Christians that evokes our Lord's invitation. These believers were too much like their environment; Laodicea was a banking centre, noted for its textile industry and famous for its eye salve (vv. 17, 18). They had become self-sufficient and self-satisfied. Now Jesus is on the outside of *his* church, so full of its own importance and so blind to its real condition. 'O wad some Pow'r the giftie gie us to see oursels as ithers see us!' wrote Rabbie Burns.[17] Well, Jesus provides the power and the gift; after all, he is 'the ruler of God's creation' (v. 14)! So he mirrors for them their condition, not so they could fall in love with their own image as in the myth of Narcissus, who gazed so long at his own reflection that he lost the will to live and died. Rather, the Lord intends that they heed his rebuke, become serious about the mess they are in and repent (v. 19).

There are various ways to handle the 'lukewarm' rebuke of verse 16. What it does *not* mean, as I have sometimes heard and perhaps in my youthful zeal preached, is that Jesus wants us totally for him (hot) or full-on against him (cold) but not sitting on the fence (lukewarm). Rather, the 'lukewarm' reference is probably to the water supply in Laodicea, which was reputedly the worst in the empire. Unlike the cold, refreshing waters found at nearby Colossae or the hot, renewing springs of Hierapolis up the road, these believers, like their water, after it had come across limestone and picked up a few other things too, were lukewarm. Inadvertently, I once put salt instead of sugar in my tea. I could not spit it out quickly enough. Unpalatable, nauseating and disgusting! That's how this church made Jesus feel.

Today, Laodicean is still a synonym for apathy, half-heartedness and sheer indifference. It conjures up all the wrong senses of being cool: chilled, unconcerned, a could-not-care-less demeanour. Contrast such an attitude to that of General William Booth, founder of The Salvation Army, who reputedly said, 'I like my religion like I like my tea – red hot!' Little wonder that The Salvation Army's flag is so evocative. The red on the flag symbolises the blood shed by Jesus Christ for our sins; the yellow proclaims the fire and power of the Holy Spirit; and the blue stands for the purity of God the Father. Such passion and commitment drove him and his early pioneers on with a holy zeal in the Army's war against sin and social evils. Sadly, such enthusiasm does not always play well with some Christians and churches. Like the passion for Jesus that was missing from both Ephesus (2:4) and here at Laodicea, it is easy to become too respectable. Yet when the Lord draws our attention to our needs and shortcomings, it is because he, the light of the world, loves us (v. 19) with a passion that took him from his throne to a cross. If lukewarm summarises you or your church's experience today, Jesus stands at the door and knocks again. Please don't keep him waiting.

Week 5

Approaching Jerusalem: unexpected heroes and villains

In this week's readings we join Luke's travelogue, as it has been called, as Jesus sets his 'face like flint' (Isaiah 50:7) and heads towards Jerusalem (Luke 9:51). Some of his ministry will be in Judea and some will take place in various towns and villages, as he resolutely makes 'his way to Jerusalem', the place that kills 'the prophets and stones those sent to you' (13:22, 34). For Jerusalem he will weep (19:41); in Jerusalem he must die (13:33), however triumphant his entry might appear (19:28). Yet beginning at Jerusalem, the gospel is to be preached to all nations (24:47).

After considering three would-be followers of Jesus, we will look at six parables that are unique to Luke, including friends who turn up at midnight, sons who wander far, and fortunes drastically changed in death. But a word of warning is perhaps appropriate about handling such stories.

The author Roald Dahl has a wonderful series of short stories called *Tales of the Unexpected*, with unforeseen twists and outcomes. Jesus' parables are often like that: we think we've got it and then suddenly there's a twist and it has us! There are two extreme positions when it comes to interpreting the parables. The comparatively modern tack says a parable can only make *one* main point. The problem is commentators often can't agree as to what it might be. The older view is that parables are extended allegories: every detail means something. Accordingly, in the tale of the good neighbour (Luke 10:25–37), for example, clearly the good Samaritan is Jesus, we are the victims, Jerusalem is heaven… well, you get the idea. The only part of the parable not usually applied in detail is the donkey – a role reserved for anyone who presses the details too far! Welcome to Unexpected Heroes and Villains.

Sunday

....

A short-sighted trio

As the time approached for him to be taken up to heaven, Jesus resolutely set out for Jerusalem. And he sent messengers on ahead, who went into a Samaritan village to get things ready for him; but the people there did not welcome him, because he was heading for Jerusalem. When the disciples James and John saw this, they asked, 'Lord, do you want us to call fire down from heaven to destroy them?' But Jesus turned and rebuked them. Then he and his disciples went to another village.

As they were walking along the road, a man said to him, 'I will follow you wherever you go.'

Jesus replied, 'Foxes have dens and birds have nests, but the Son of Man has no place to lay his head.'

He said to another man, 'Follow me.'

But he replied, 'Lord, first let me go and bury my father.'

Jesus said to him, 'Let the dead bury their own dead, but you go and proclaim the kingdom of God.'

Still another said, 'I will follow you, Lord; but first let me go back and say goodbye to my family.'

Jesus replied, 'No one who puts a hand to the plough and looks back is fit for service in the kingdom of God.'

LUKE 9:51–62

It was a domestic flight into London Heathrow Airport and I had a mere 25 minutes to catch the late-night bus back to the south coast. I positioned myself right at the back of the plane, so that when the rear exit opened I would be off and, just having hand luggage, I would be in time to catch my coach. Okay, the plane was five minutes late, but

I still had enough time. We landed, the front door was opened on the plane but the rear door wasn't. I was last off (something about the first being last was beginning to echo through my brain). I sprinted to the bus station and there to my delight was my coach – but slowly crawling away from the terminus! I had missed it by seconds, and National Express seems to have a policy that if I am not there, its coaches leave without me.

In this passage, as Jesus begins his long and tortuous journey to Jerusalem (vv. 51, 53), we encounter three would-be disciples who all miss Christ's gospel bus. Today, there are many people who think that if they only had a personal encounter with Jesus in some miraculous way, then they would become Christians. However, the gospels remind us constantly, and here is a case in point, that it is possible to see Jesus, meet Jesus and hear Jesus and still not follow him.

Take the first man, for instance. We might call him Mr Too Hot. To be enthusiastic and deeply committed to the cause of Jesus Christ is highly desirable and commendable. This man's problem was of a different sort. He had failed to count the cost, as Jesus will illustrate in a subsequent parable (Luke 14:28). So, the Lord spells out some of the hardships of following him: far from discipleship being a way to feather our nests and build a nest egg, unlike the birds of the air, he and by implication his followers might have to rough it (v. 58). So, count the cost.

At the other extreme is Mr Ice Cold. This time, Jesus takes the initiative and calls him in words that are precisely the same as the call, for example, to Levi the taxman, who 'got up, left everything and followed him' (Luke 5:27, 28). At first blush, the reply of Mr Ice Cold seems very reasonable, for he has a father to bury. Given the cultural background, however, his words probably mean 'whenever my father has died, and I have tidied everything up, then that will be the time to follow you'. The author H.G. Wells spent three of his teenage years as an unhappy apprentice draper, working 13-hour days and sleeping in a dormitory with the other apprentices. One day, he felt a massive compulsion to 'get out immediately'. He did, and became the famous and prolific author we know. Of course, Levi did so too. Didn't he go on to write one of the gospels? So, here's another lesson: proclaim the kingdom (v. 60) – and do it now!

In between our two characters, Hot and Cold, seems to sit Mr Lukewarm. Again, on the surface the request seems very reasonable. Like a soldier on active service called away to duty, aren't some fond farewells in order before leaving for battle? But our Lord's word about putting our hands to the plough and looking back (v. 62) – a very stupid thing to do if we want to plough in straight lines – suggests the kind of man who, when asked if he was indecisive, replied, 'Well, yes and no!' One familiar Cockney song, written in 1919, reminds the wife, as a couple are moving home: 'Don't dilly-dally on the way'. Here is someone distracted, procrastinating when decisive action is called for, dilly-dallying when Christ is passing by. As I write, President Donald Trump has been appointing his cabinet and advisers. Some of them are incredibly high-powered people, in well-paid roles with secure jobs and futures. But they have received a presidential invitation! Their rewards for responding are unclear, beyond the privilege of serving their president and country. No one, however, can match what Jesus offers: 'Your names are written in heaven'. Little wonder he tells his followers to 'rejoice' (Luke 10:20)!

Samaritans

On one occasion an expert in the law stood up to test Jesus. 'Teacher,' he asked, 'what must I do to inherit eternal life?'

'What is written in the Law?' he replied. 'How do you read it?'

He answered, '"Love the Lord your God with all your heart and with all your soul and with all your strength and with all your mind"; and, "Love your neighbour as yourself."'

'You have answered correctly,' Jesus replied. 'Do this and you will live.'

But he wanted to justify himself, so he asked Jesus, 'And who is my neighbour?'

In reply Jesus said: 'A man was going down from Jerusalem to Jericho, when he was attacked by robbers. They stripped him of his clothes, beat him and went away, leaving him half-dead. A priest happened to be going down the same road, and when he saw the man, he passed by on the other side. So too, a Levite, when he came to the place and saw him, passed by on the other side. But a Samaritan, as he travelled, came where the man was; and when he saw him, he took pity on him. He went to him and bandaged his wounds, pouring on oil and wine. Then he put the man on his own donkey, brought him to an inn and took care of him. The next day he took out two denarii and gave them to the innkeeper. "Look after him," he said, "and when I return, I will reimburse you for any extra expense you may have."

'Which of these three do you think was a neighbour to the man who fell into the hands of robbers?'

> The expert in the law replied, 'The one who had mercy on
> him.'
> Jesus told him, 'Go and do likewise.'
> LUKE 10:25–37

Just about everyone's heard the story of the good Samaritan. Even
those who are a little hazy about its details are probably aware of
the Samaritans, the organisation set up in 1953 by Chad Varah, an
Anglican vicar, to offer help to those contemplating suicide or feeling
themselves drowning in the desperate straits of life. As for this story
from Jesus, surely its meaning is abundantly clear – be a good
neighbour. So, let's be good Samaritans and help folk who struggle
along life's road, right?

This parable, however, can easily fall victim to the twin extremes
I mentioned in the introduction to this week's meditations: an
extended allegory type of interpretation or the one main lesson kind
– be a good neighbour! Accordingly, the first approach has even been
used to work out the date of the second coming of Jesus. How? Well,
the two denarii are the equivalent of two days' worth of wages. We
are told that a day is as a thousand years with the Lord (2 Peter 3:8).
So, in around 2,000 years Jesus will return – any time now, by 2030
perhaps? Check out Mark 13:32 if you find that persuasive! I have
already mentioned the 'donkey approach' in the introduction.

On the other side, if it is about being a good neighbour, and we hear
Jesus saying 'Go and do likewise' (v. 37), there are problems too.
Have we never passed by someone in need? In its haunting lyrics,
'Another Day in Paradise' portrays an old woman living rough on the
streets, and the person she asks for help simply pretends he does
not hear her as he goes whistling on his way. So, why is this not
the main point of the parable? Because the context of the parable
is not *primarily* about being a good neighbour but in answer to the
question, 'What must I do to inherit eternal life?' (v. 25). Jesus asks
how the questioner reads the law and affirms his correct reply: love
God and your neighbour. But the man, wishing 'to justify himself'

(v. 29), asks a follow-up question about 'who is my neighbour?' The parable illustrates a works religion, where we hope, when weighed in the scales, that our good deeds outweigh our bad. If we want eternal life, we are going to have to work for it! The trouble is, no one has kept all the golden rules or ever done enough, so we are lost. In one fell swoop of a parable, we have overturned the whole gospel of God's grace.

At another level of interpretation, however, Jesus may be viewed as the good Samaritan, the despised outsider who does indeed come to us in our beat-up, broken state. The storyline is that Jesus is on his way to Jerusalem to die, becoming the saviour of the world, granting remission of sins to all who believe. Jesus becomes the neighbour to me in all my need. In the words of Paul, 'it is by grace you have been saved… not by works, so that no one can boast' (Ephesians 2:8–9).

Good! So that's us off the sharp hook of loving our neighbour. If I am saved by grace, doesn't that mean that like the priest I can walk by on the other side of the street, ignoring human need? Those verses in Ephesians also have a context. The next verse tells us that we have been created in Christ 'to do good works' (v. 10) that God has pre-planned for us! Here's the paradox in this familiar story. Don't for one moment let us imagine we could ever be such wonderful 24/7 neighbours, loving others as much as we love ourselves, and then thinking that will be the basis on which eternal life will be ours. On the other hand, recognising 'the gift of God is eternal life in Christ Jesus our Lord' (Romans 6:23), we are set free to love God and others. One day, by God's grace, it will eternally be 'another day in paradise'. With such a prospect in view, let's go and make someone's day everyday. Samaritans do that sort of thing!

Tuesday

A midnight caller

Then Jesus said to them, 'Suppose you have a friend, and you go to him at midnight and say, 'Friend, lend me three loaves of bread; a friend of mine on a journey has come to me, and I have no food to offer him.' And suppose the one inside answers, 'Don't bother me. The door is already locked, and my children and I are in bed. I can't get up and give you anything.' I tell you, even though he will not get up and give you the bread because of friendship, yet because of your shameless audacity he will surely get up and give you as much as you need.

LUKE 11:5–8

Midnight Caller was a US TV series produced between 1988 and 1991, and ran to 61 episodes. Jack Killian is the host, 'The Nighthawk', of an overnight radio talk show in which he listens to people's difficulties, shares some of his own and, using his background as a former detective, solves some of their problems during the day. In this parable, we meet a midnight caller who does not seem to be too bothered about who he upsets so long as he gets what he needs.

The story here is, at one level, straightforward. It's about prayer, and it is given in the context of what is known as the Lord's Prayer (the prayer Jesus gave not the prayer he prayed). That prayer, though brief, is all-encompassing, covering all the bases. It starts with God the Father and his honour and coming kingdom. It proceeds with requests for our physical, spiritual and moral needs. It is indeed a pattern for our praying. Which parts do you most frequently pray? What areas do you find yourself struggling with? And do you notice how plural pronouns are used: *our* daily bread; *our* sins; against *us*; lead *us* not into temptation? Surely the implication of those plurals is that we need to pray with others as well as individually. Often others are used to answer the request, 'Lord, teach *us* to pray' (v. 1). I am grateful for what I have learned from many different Christians who have been taught by Jesus in the school of prayer.

The midnight caller story accurately mirrors life in Israel's villages, where folk often lived on the breadline, hence the prayer for 'daily bread' (v. 3). Nevertheless, hospitality was a sacred duty if a family member or messenger arrived. Sadly, how relevant the picture is for vast amounts of people who today live on or have gone over the edge of poverty. What happens when the unexpected visitor arrives? Metaphorically, what do we do when the unforeseen shows up not as a friend at midnight but a life-threatening enemy? An illness strikes; a redundancy occurs; a family crisis happens. Where do we find the resources to cope? The challenge here is, do we know where and to whom to turn? Clearly the first man in the parable did, for the story turns on knowing where to get bread, especially at midnight. The message in its context is that we should go to the Lord for what he alone can provide, since he is a 'how much more' God (v. 13). Increasingly, however, we live in a culture where God, if thought to exist, is viewed as the last-chance saloon.

Is that help reluctantly given by the one being shaken out of bed at midnight? Traditionally, the interpretation is that the Lord himself appears to have a reluctance that needs to be overcome by the asking, seeking and knocking that Jesus refers to (vv. 9–10). True, some prayers never 'raise God' because they are too flippant: we do not really mean them. However, in this story, the man outside does mean business – he is bold and persistent (v. 8). He keeps asking until he receives. Have you had any persistent requests recently answered?

But there is another possible interpretation. The word translated 'shameless audacity' in verse 8 might point to the man knocking at the door – he's shameless in his request. But given the honour culture of village life in first-century Israel, it likely refers to the householder, who wishes to 'preserve his good name' (NIV footnote). His reputation is on the line: he will be bad-mouthed if he does not help. So, to avoid the shame he does the necessary. Now the parable is not so much a call to persistence, though that is not ruled out, but a reminder that if a householder has a reputation to guard and therefore helps a friend, our Father in heaven is a 'how much more' God of kindness and love. His reputation is tied up with hearing the prayers of his children. And what he provides is not only bread for the body but the most indispensable gift of all, his Holy Spirit (v. 13).

What was a little opaque about Jack Killian's lifestyle in *Midnight Caller* was his ability to be up all night and then sort out people's problems during the day. When did he sleep? But that's TV. What is not opaque here is God's willingness to hear the prayers of his people when the expected and the unexpected arrive. The reluctance is often on our side, not his. In his hauntingly beautiful 'Sanctuary', based on Psalm 73, Marty Goetz probes our reluctance to come to the Lord, when he sings of sensing the reality of God yet being so reluctant to come to him.

It's always time for a midnight call on our Father, whatever time of day it may be.

Amazing grace

Jesus continued: 'There was a man who had two sons. The younger one said to his father, "Father, give me my share of the estate." So he divided his property between them.

'Not long after that, the younger son got together all he had, set off for a distant country and there squandered his wealth in wild living. After he had spent everything, there was a severe famine in that whole country, and he began to be in need. So he went and hired himself out to a citizen of that country, who sent him to his fields to feed pigs. He longed to fill his stomach with the pods that the pigs were eating, but no one gave him anything.

'When he came to his senses, he said, "How many of my father's hired servants have food to spare, and here I am starving to death! I will set out and go back to my father and say to him: Father, I have sinned against heaven and against you. I am no longer worthy to be called your son; make me like one of your hired servants." So he got up and went to his father.

'But while he was still a long way off, his father saw him and was filled with compassion for him; he ran to his son, threw his arms round him and kissed him.

'The son said to him, "Father, I have sinned against heaven and against you. I am no longer worthy to be called your son."

'But the father said to his servants, "Quick! Bring the best robe and put it on him. Put a ring on his finger and sandals on his feet. Bring the fattened calf and kill it. Let's have a feast and celebrate. For this son of mine was dead and is alive again; he was lost and is found." So they began to celebrate...

'The elder brother became angry and refused to go in. So his father went out and pleaded with him. But he answered his father, "Look! All these years I've been slaving for you and never disobeyed your orders. Yet you never gave me even a young goat so I could celebrate with my friends. But when this son of yours who has squandered your property with prostitutes comes home, you kill the fattened calf for him!"

'"My son," the father said, "you are always with me, and everything I have is yours. But we had to celebrate and be glad, because this brother of yours was dead and is alive again; he was lost and is found."'

LUKE 15:11–32

Along with the good Samaritan, this is the best known of Jesus' parables. Its ability to resonate with people of all types and ages, across cultures and down the centuries, is because so many of us have been prodigals too, in thought if not in deed. And its themes of grace and redemption are echoed continually in art, music and literature. For every family somewhere has the proverbial black sheep, the one who is incommunicado and literally or metaphorically in the 'distant country' (v. 13). Hardly a week goes by when I am not speaking with some parent in pain for a daughter whose once bright faith is no more or a son who kicked over the traces and fell into an ever-downward spiral of sex, drugs and rock 'n' roll. Of course, many single people I chat to likewise carry heavy hearts and a thousand regrets for a family member, dad, sister, grandparent. What is to be said and done?

First, acknowledge that prodigals appear in the best of families. Some of today's pop psychology might suggest that the hero of the story was the erring son himself. Obviously, he was living in a strict and asphyxiating environment; clearly, the father figure was far too domineering and the boy needed to break free and find himself. There are indeed such homes and parents – C.S. Lewis made the marvellous quip about such parental control: 'She's the sort of woman who lives for others – you can always tell the others by their hunted expression.'[18] The bottom line in this story, however, is that there was nothing wrong with the father. No parent or home is perfect. I have met countless parents laden with false guilt because, although they did their best, their child still strayed. It happens. Life generally and children particularly do not come with money-back guarantees.

One writer called this story *The Waiting Father*.[19] That does not stop our going to seek out the erring child: the previous parables in this chapter of lost sheep and silver make that abundantly clear. But there are many situations where patience (and prayer) is the only way forward. It's tempting to rush in where angels fear to tread or to let the prodigal know how much they have let the family down and how grateful they ought to be. Wiser to wait for the 'famine' to hit, the penny to drop, and the prodigal to acknowledge how good dad and home are (v. 17).

What then? As somebody quipped, 'Pray that when the prodigal returns home, the first person they meet is not the elder brother!' There's an 'elder brother' in all our hearts too. A major point of this *Tale of the Unexpected* is that one of the great dangers for nice, respectable, stay-at-home-and-never-wandered-far people is elder-brother smug self-righteousness. We look down on others – check out the contrasting attitudes of the Pharisee and tax collector at Luke 18:9–14.

Before concluding that this story is mainly about fixing broken families and fractured relationships, all on the horizontal plane, it would be folly to miss the vertical dimension – our estrangement from God the Father. It is possible to either wander far from God and live riotously in the 'distant country' or stay at home and be equally lost. We need both brothers on stage to understand the story. Over a century ago and for nearly 20 years, Sam Hadley was the superintendent of the Water Street Mission, New York, a rescue mission for life's prodigals. One day, a young man turned up who'd been on the streets for a few days, having run away from home.

The story unfolded over a bowl of soup. He had stolen some money from his father's shop, headed for the racetrack and lost the lot. Sam eventually got his permission to contact his dad by telegram, the quickest form of communication in those days, though the boy was unsure how his father would react. Just before the evening service began, a telegraph boy entered the mission: 'Telegram! Telegram for Mr Hadley!' Sam opened it, read it and passed it to the young prodigal. It contained just four words: COME HOME. YOUR FATHER. The wonderful gospel of Jesus welcomes us back to God, whether we have been in the far country or lost at home, and it has the power to restore and heal broken lives and relationships on earth too. May all our prodigals soon come home, including those wanderers found in our own hearts, for Jesus' sake!

....

Future shock

'There was a rich man who was dressed in purple and fine linen and lived in luxury every day. At his gate was laid a beggar named Lazarus, covered with sores and longing to eat what fell from the rich man's table. Even the dogs came and licked his sores.

'The time came when the beggar died and the angels carried him to Abraham's side. The rich man also died and was buried. In Hades, where he was in torment, he looked up and saw Abraham far away, with Lazarus by his side. So he called to him, "Father Abraham, have pity on me and send Lazarus to dip the tip of his finger in water and cool my tongue, because I am in agony in this fire."

'But Abraham replied, "Son, remember that in your lifetime you received your good things, while Lazarus received bad things, but now he is comforted here and you are in agony. And besides all this, between us and you a great chasm has been set in place, so that those who want to go from here to you cannot, nor can anyone cross over from there to us."

'He answered, "Then I beg you, father, send Lazarus to my family, for I have five brothers. Let him warn them, so that they will not also come to this place of torment."

'Abraham replied, "They have Moses and the Prophets; let them listen to them."

'"No, father Abraham," he said, "but if someone from the dead goes to them, they will repent."

'He said to him, "If they do not listen to Moses and the Prophets, they will not be convinced even if someone rises from the dead."'

LUKE 16:19–31

Nearly 50 years ago, Alvin Toffler wrote the bestseller *Future Shock*, a book that sought to predict tomorrow's world from today's trends. It has spawned a whole industry for anticipating movements economically, politically and socially. 'Future shock' aptly summarises this tale of massive role reversal, as we hear a voice from beyond the grave. Yet we approach the story cautiously, recognising its parabolic elements. We explore three questions that the narrative should raise in our minds.

Is it a true-to-life story?

Who would deny that this parable mirrors life, ancient and modern, and is a commentary on social injustice and poverty? On the one side is a wealthy man, beautifully attired and living in a large house with its impressive portico (vv. 19–20). Jesus' parables often speak about our wealth, and its dangers and opportunities. After death, in a place of torment (v. 23), he is reminded by Abraham that 'in your lifetime you received *your* good things' (v. 25, emphasis added). The 'your' is significant. When we have money, it is easy to fall into the trap of thinking it is ours, instead of merely loaned for a while. Our lives, even in Lent, may find it hard to break away from 'my', 'mine' and 'me' words – 'aggressive' not possessive pronouns, as a little boy called them.

On the other side of his gate a beggar was laid, presumably disabled and covered with sores, starving and desperately longing for some crumbs from his table. The plight of starving and malnourished children on our TV screens should draw forth 'the milk of human kindness', but when ignored such milk can sour in our souls and shrivel our humanity. It was the latter effect on the rich man who every day failed to show anything of the love of God expressed in kindness to his neighbour. Is there a beggar at your gate today? Someone in emotional, financial or spiritual poverty? A family member? Someone unvisited and friendless in a senior citizen's home near you? Is there a 'beggar' you could help this week?

Is it a true after-life story?

Did Jesus tell this story to satisfy our curiosity on the post-mortem state? Granted caution in not pressing every detail, two points should be clear: the dark side of hope and the bright side of darkness. On the dark side, the story seems to portray some form of an intermediate state between death and the general resurrection, since the man's brothers are still living on earth (v. 28). So, the rich man is in Hades (v. 23), not Gehenna, the place of final judgement. Does that lessen the lesson here? We might hope that everyone will be safe on the other side, but the Bible does not teach a universalism that everyone and everything will be well, regardless of repentance and faith. The inference is that our destinies are fixed at death, barred by an impassable 'great chasm' (v. 26). Death does not change our characters. The rich man still treated the beggar as an errand boy: 'Send Lazarus to dip the tip of his finger in water… send Lazarus to my family' (vv. 24, 27). He died as self-centredly as he lived. Many of us find all this so difficult, and if it were not for Jesus, love incarnate, telling us starkly about such things we might turn away. There is, thankfully, the bright side of darkness, for Lazarus goes to 'Abraham's side' (v. 22). Told before the pivotal events of Easter, Jesus necessarily speaks in Old Testament terms. So what happens now to a believer in death? 'Today you will be with me in paradise' (Luke 23:43) is uttered to a penitent, dying thief; departing this life to 'be with Christ' is how the apostle expresses it, safe in Jesus (Philippians 1:23).

Our life story?

The story should shock us into reflecting seriously on our own life story. Are we prepared for death? It can come at any time, whether we are 18 or 88. But we mishandle this story if we conclude that heaven and hell are simply about reversing life's fortunes. The beggar's name, Lazarus, holds a clue: it means 'God is my helper'. Our circumstances, whether I am rich or poor, in fine fettle or suffering terribly, can either drive us to God for mercy or away from him. The rich can live for God; the poor may hate God for their lot – and vice versa. The enduring point is that our position in life, favoured or in want, is no guide to where we spend eternity. So, how can we know? We need to take the positive from Abraham's rebuke: 'If they do not listen to Moses and the Prophets, they will not be convinced even if someone rises from the dead' (v. 31). Someone has risen from the dead, as the resurrection demonstrates. Scripture proclaims Jesus as the way from this world to the next, from death to life. Some years ago, the golfer Seve Ballesteros appeared in an American Express advert: 'Don't leave home without it!' was his punchline. Forget Alvin Toffler! To die without Christ opens us to real *future shock*. Forget the American Express card: don't leave life without Christ.

Open all hours?

> 'Suppose one of you has a servant ploughing or looking after
> the sheep. Will he say to the servant when he comes in from
> the field, "Come along now and sit down to eat?" Won't he
> rather say, "Prepare my supper, get yourself ready and wait
> on me while I eat and drink; after that you may eat and
> drink?" Will he thank the servant because he did what he was
> told to do? So you also, when you have done everything you
> were told to do, should say, "We are unworthy servants; we
> have only done our duty."'
>
> LUKE 17:7–10

If Marx and Engels' *Communist Manifesto*, with its famous slogan
'Workers of the world, unite! You have nothing to lose but your
chains!', had not helped to inspire the 1917 Bolshevik Revolution in
Russia, at first blush this story could have. It seems so shocking: work
your socks off, slaving all day. Then come home and work all night for
a master whose only compliment is that you merely did your duty.
When that's done, beat yourself up a little more by telling yourself
how unworthy you are. That seems to be grist to the mill, driving us
to the conclusion that such characterises our service for the Lord.
Working 24/7 isn't enough for him! Even if it was, we are so unworthy
anyway. Doesn't that project an image of God as a demanding
tyrant? Some background may put things into perspective.

There were two kinds of servant in the Bible. The casual day-labourer
was economically vulnerable, being hired day-to-day (Matthew
20:1–16). Then there was the slave, someone who either had been
sold or had sold themselves into slavery. At the heart of such an

arrangement was the acceptance of a master's total authority. The Bible seems to take slavery for granted. Nowhere are masters told to manumit slaves or are slaves called to rebel. Is that a surprise? On the other hand, in the Christian household reciprocal obligations are laid on both slaves and masters (Ephesians 6:5–9; Colossians 3:22, 4:1). That was a revolutionary concept! Moreover, many slaves gladly stayed with a master they loved (Exodus 21:2–6). In other words, a relationship of mutual trust, dependence and affection could blossom. A slave was often far better off than a day-labourer, because they had security and worth if they belonged to a good master.

The parable reads as if a demanding despot is seeking to get his pound of flesh out of his slave. In fact, even modest households had slaves. They worked the fields, herded the animals, cooked, took the children to school, and so on. It was generally reasonable service. In addition, the meal in the story is not a 'dinner at eight', but something around 3.00 pm. A slave in Israel never worked 24/7: the Sabbath saw to that (Exodus 20:8). The point in this story is that the slave has done what could reasonably be expected. If he had, does that place the master in the slave's debt?

It all hangs on the meaning of 'Will he thank the servant?' (v. 9). An employer, parent or coach is wise to regularly thank folk for what they do, but if I do for God what is reasonably expected of me, does he have to thank me because he owes me – that promotion, this healing, that answer to prayer? It is the kind of thing we say generally: 'after all I did for that organisation'. As the Bible keeps reminding us, however, God owes no one anything, while we owe him everything. A more literal rendering of the conversation says, 'we are servants who have no need' (v. 10). In other words, 'Lord, you owe us nothing; we've merely done our duty.'

So, when we have done our reasonable bit, what then? Are we to expect a round of applause? 'Will he say to the servant... "Come along now and sit down to eat"?' (v. 7). Would we expect the master to do that? The expected answer is 'No!' Is the major point, therefore, to remain sweet, trust to God's grace and never presume on it or to think that God owes us?

In Luke 12:35–38, we find a master who has his faithful servants 'recline at the table', and he serves them! There's the stark reminder that we are servants of a gracious master who himself became the servant, and through his service of sacrifice manumits slaves of sin not only to be his servants but his sons and daughters. Many episodes of the BBC sitcom *Open All Hours* were rounded off by the main character, Arkwright, reflecting on his day and telling the Lord all about it. A great idea 24/7!

Saturday

....

What's so dangerous about grace?

While they were listening to this, he went on to tell them a parable, because he was near Jerusalem and the people thought that the kingdom of God was going to appear at once. He said: 'A man of noble birth went to a distant country to have himself appointed king and then to return. So he called ten of his servants and gave them ten minas. "Put this money to work," he said, "until I come back."

'But his subjects hated him and sent a delegation after him to say, "We don't want this man to be our king."

'He was made king, however, and returned home. Then he sent for the servants to whom he had given the money, in order to find out what they had gained with it.

'The first one came and said, "Sir, your mina has earned ten more."

'"Well done, my good servant!" his master replied. "Because you have been trustworthy in a very small matter, take charge of ten cities."

'The second came and said, "Sir, your mina has earned five more."

'His master answered, "You take charge of five cities."

'Then another servant came and said, "Sir, here is your mina; I have kept it laid away in a piece of cloth. I was afraid of you, because you are a hard man. You take out what you did not put in and reap what you did not sow."

'His master replied, "I will judge you by your own words, you wicked servant! You knew, did you, that I am a hard man, taking out what I did not put in, and reaping what I did not sow? Why then didn't you put my money on deposit, so that when I came back, I could have collected it with interest?"

'Then he said to those standing by, "Take his mina away from him and give it to the one who has ten minas."

'"Sir," they said, "he already has ten!"

'He replied, "I tell you that to everyone who has, more will be given, but as for the one who has nothing, even what they have will be taken away. But those enemies of mine who did not want me to be king over them – bring them here and kill them in front of me."

LUKE 19:11-27

Did you know that grace is not only amazing but also dangerous? Christians believe in grace, God's unmerited favour towards humanity through Jesus Christ. It is 'amazing grace', as these parables of Jesus remind us in different and complementary ways. They highlight outcast Samaritans (ch. 10), recalcitrant sons (ch. 15), shady dealers (ch. 16) and annoying widows (ch. 18). *Les Misérables*, Victor Hugo's famous historical novel adapted into a hit musical, also provides a long illustration of grace, telling the story of what happens to a poor, undeserving felon, Valjean, when he is shown grace by a Christian bishop. Why, then, is grace also dangerous?

One answer is that we might jump to the wrong conclusions, deducing that if we are shown God's grace then it is like the 'get out of jail free' card in the boardgame *Monopoly*, giving us another chance to live and behave like we always have. That folly is illustrated by the man who, entrusted with one mina, 'kept it laid away in a piece of cloth' (v. 20). The Bible everywhere insists that God's salvation is a free gift for penitents who ask for mercy, as Luke repeatedly shows (15:18–19; 18:13). It is purchased by his infinite love demonstrated through the life and death of Christ, so it can't be *earned*. But it can be *evidenced*, as we see in the conversion of Zacchaeus (19:1–10). Clearly, this man in the parable, like the other nine given a single mina, the equivalent of about three months' wages, failed to evidence any saving grace. The rest did, some better than others, and were suitably rewarded (vv. 16–19). His problem? He had a completely wrong-headed view of the master. Indeed, what he says is massively insulting, the word 'hard' being a translation of the Greek word *austeros* – severe, strict, grave. And he backs up his accusation with a further insult about his master taking more than he gives (v. 21). In the context, of course, this comes down to a view of God that explains the man's actions or lack of them. He's got the wrong God! He had forgotten what he had been given in the first place.

The apostle Paul rhetorically asks, 'Shall we go on sinning so that grace may increase?' (Romans 6:1). For there have always been people, then and now, who imagine the answer is, 'Yes! We can do what we like; we're made that way. And, after all, it's God's job to forgive, so let's keep him busy!' The Bible recognises that it's possible to 'turn the grace of God into a licence' (Jude 4), and presume that grace is given so that I can do life my way. The truth is that God's astounding grace, which offers salvation to all, 'teaches us to say "No" to ungodliness… and to live self-controlled, upright and godly lives' (Titus 2:12). To misunderstand the purpose of grace shown can be literally fatal. For example, when the loveable, alcoholic, world-famous footballer George Best was controversially given a liver transplant, the medical team's hope was presumably that he would change his lifestyle, curbing his alcohol intake. Sadly, he didn't, his problems returned and he died a mere three years later. Tragic.

The tragedy of one-mina man was that of a wasted life. Instead of seeing the grace of what he had received as a stimulus to action, it became the cause of his indolence, exhibiting 'contempt for the riches of his kindness' and failing to recognise 'that God's kindness is intended to lead… to repentance' (Romans 2:4). In contrast, Victor Hugo's Valjean did grasp the implications of grace. Grace changed his life and, in turn, the lives of others. *Les Misérables*, of course, is fiction, but isn't it a fact that we all need God's grace to meet us as and where we are, and change us into what we should be? Such transformation is a process, not something instantaneous.

In responding to God's grace, Christ's followers become those who are more honest, more authentic, more vulnerable, more humble, more real, more human, more industrious and more useful. In a phrase, we are to become 'more like Jesus'. Such people stand away from the crowd, stand up for Jesus and stand out as bearers of the grace of God to others. Such lives challenge the status quo and the accepted wisdom of an age where, for many, God either does not exist or is not worth too much attention. Christians are called upon to 'become blameless and pure, "children of God without fault in a warped and crooked generation." Then you will shine among them like stars in the sky as you hold firmly to the word of life' (Philippians 2:15–16). Such people are countercultural, and their godliness really is dangerous. How needed they are!

Week 6

....

Redeeming the world: the unrecognised builder

Years ago, there was a nicely produced Easter leaflet entitled 'Three Days That Shook the World'. Its focus was on what we call Good Friday, Holy Saturday and Easter Sunday. It made its points well, as I recall, but it did not go far enough (to be fair, that was not its intention). Over the next nine days, we will see a huge picture emerging from Good Friday, Holy Saturday and Easter Sunday.

The whole mission and purpose of our Lord's coming as a babe, a man, a preacher, a healer and a redeemer who comes 'to seek and save the lost' (Luke 19:10) now comes to fulfilment. The holy city of Jerusalem is anything but. He weeps for it, highlights its corruption in its treatment of the vulnerable, predicts its destruction, suffers death within it, rises triumphantly from it, and tells his disciples to remain in it until, clothed with power, they can take his good news to every city, town, people and nation. More than three days, for sure. And what days they are! They not only shook the world but will continue to do so until the carpenter-builder's rebuilding job is complete.

The words of the chorus that accompanied a popular hymn of yesteryear help focus us on the essential tools of Christ's trade:

Living, He loved me; dying, He saved me,
Buried, He carried my sins far away;
Rising, He justified, freely for ever:
One day He's coming – O glorious day!

J. Wilbur Chapman (1859–1918)

Palm Sunday

Crossing the Rubicon

After Jesus had said this, he went on ahead, going up to Jerusalem. As he approached Bethphage and Bethany at the hill called the Mount of Olives, he sent two of his disciples, saying to them, 'Go to the village ahead of you, and as you enter it, you will find a colt tied there, which no one has ever ridden. Untie it and bring it here.

When he came near the place where the road goes down the Mount of Olives, the whole crowd of disciples began joyfully to praise God in loud voices for all the miracles they had seen:
   'Blessed is the king who comes in the name of the Lord!'
   'Peace in heaven and glory in the highest!'

As he approached Jerusalem and saw the city, he wept over it and said, 'If you, even you, had only known on this day what would bring you peace – but now it is hidden from your eyes.'
LUKE 19:28–30, 37–38, 41–42

In 49BC, Julius Caesar marched with his army from Cisalpine Gaul and crossed a little stream in northern Italy, the Rubicon. The crossing was both literal and symbolic, for it was a declaration of war on the Roman Republic, an act of rebellion and treason. No turning back now, the Rubicon had been crossed. On a spring day some 80 years later, Jesus left the village of Bethany, two miles east of Jerusalem, mounted a colt and rode into that city with a crowd waving palm branches not swords. No turning back now, his Rubicon had been crossed, an action full of metaphor and symbolism as he declared a different kind of war on the republic of sin and darkness.

Although all the Gospels record the triumphal entry of Jesus, it is only Luke who adds the telling postscript, 'As he approached Jerusalem and saw the city, he wept over it' (v. 41). These days, halfway up the Mount of Olives stands the beautiful church of Dominus Flevit, designed by the Italian architect Antonio Barluzzi and constructed between 1953 and 1955. It is constructed in the shape of a teardrop, for it was here, as the Latin name indicates, 'the Lord wept'. Why his tears?

Palm Sunday – so-called because John describes the crowd taking 'palm branches' to meet Jesus (John 12:13) – invests this entry with royal significance: 'Blessed is the king who comes in the name of the Lord' (v. 38; 2 Kings 9:13). The king has come to his city! Here's an event not merely of historical moment but cosmic significance. *Prophetically*, Zechariah had foreseen it over 500 years before (Zechariah 9:9); God's plans and purposes are formed not only from 'long ages past' (Romans 16:25) but 'before the creation of the world' (Ephesians 1:4). *Publicly*, Christ's entry underlined the fact that Christian faith is not some esoteric religion, like many cults ancient and modern. In the memorable words of Paul to King Agrippa, Christianity is public domain, for 'it was not done in a corner' (Acts 26:26). And Jesus unlike Caesar comes *peacefully*, on a colt not a warhorse, not to destroy but to reconcile people to God. So, why the tears?

Life can be full of 'what might have beens'. Herein lies the tragedy and the tears of the triumphal entry. Opportunity is knocking as the Lord draws near, only to be met by the blindness and stubbornness of the human heart: 'If you, even you, had only known on this day what would bring you peace – but now it is hidden from your eyes… you did not recognise the time of God's coming to you' (vv. 42, 44). 'Hidden' – is that God's fault? Earlier in the gospel, the Lord had expressed his pain over this recalcitrant city: 'Jerusalem, Jerusalem, you who kill the prophets and stone those sent to you, how often I have longed to gather your children together, as a hen gathers her chicks under her wings, and you were not willing' (13:34). How damning those words, 'you were not willing'. I think it was the great missionary to India, Dr E. Stanley Jones, who somewhere remarked that we control our choices but we can't control the consequences of those choices.

When blind Bartimaeus, sitting near Jericho, a city once marked out for destruction (Joshua 6), heard that 'Jesus of Nazareth is passing by', he recognised the time of God's coming, cried out for mercy and was miraculously healed (Luke 18:35–43). Likewise, the untrustworthy and rich tax collector, Zacchaeus, also from Jericho, seized his opportunity for God's coming, repented and gladly welcomed the Jesus who came 'to seek and to save the lost' (Luke 19:1–10). How ironic that when the long-expected Messiah comes to his holy city, in contrast to the putative unholiness of Jericho, the latter welcomes him and the former ultimately rejects him. And the result was catastrophic devastation for that ancient city within 40 years, underlined in verses 43 and 44, and amplified in chapter 21, as we will see.

The other day, I heard a remarkable story of a recently discovered rich vein of gold in the Antipodes. I don't know if it could be classed as insider trading or just being speculative, but the opportunity to buy shares in this gold mine was presented to a man before the news broke. He prevaricated. The £20,000 buy-in was, he felt, too risky. A few days later, the shares rocketed and he might now have been a millionaire. He can't stop kicking himself. In the words of Brutus to Cassius in Shakespeare's *Julius Caesar*, 'There is a tide in the affairs of men, which taken at the flood, leads on to fortune. Omitted, all the voyage of their life is bound in shallows and in miseries' (Act IV, sc. iii). Regret is often a synonym for opportunity having knocked and been ignored. The opportunity to invest in the pure gold of Christ was rejected by Jerusalem. Little wonder Jesus wept as it remained blind and judgement came. That was its story. God forbid it should be ours.

....

Givers and takers

While all the people were listening, Jesus said to his disciples, 'Beware of the teachers of the law. They like to walk around in flowing robes and love to be greeted with respect in the market-places and have the most important seats in the synagogues and the places of honour at banquets. They devour widows' houses and for a show make lengthy prayers. These men will be punished most severely.'

As Jesus looked up, he saw the rich putting their gifts into the temple treasury. He also saw a poor widow put in two very small copper coins. 'Truly I tell you,' he said, 'this poor widow has put in more than all the others. All these people gave their gifts out of their wealth; but she out of her poverty put in all she had to live on.'

LUKE 20:45–21:4

Recently, the elderly wife of a retired vicar was contacted by phone about their bank accounts. Everything seemed rather convincing, and she duly transferred over £20,000 to a more secure account. It was a complete scam, but as she had agreed to do it, there was no recourse to law. Every day, young and old alike are cheated out of their possessions, and sometimes their innocence, by shrewd and merciless operators. It is especially reprehensible when the person scammed is 'a vulnerable adult', for which there is in English law no precise definition. However, when someone especially vulnerable is ripped off, there is often outrage expressed by their community and a 'serves them right' attitude when the perpetrators are brought to justice.

Lest we wonder why money should get a look-in during Passion week, we do well to remember the massive number of things Jesus had to say about its uses and abuses. Indeed, the corrupt nature of religion is once again exposed by this part of the Passion narrative, as vulnerable widows are exploited. What heightens the feelings of disgust about their exploitation is that it was being carried out under a cloak of religious piety by those who 'devour widows' houses and for a show make lengthy prayers' (v. 47). How did that happen? The clue is in the phrase 'the teachers of the law' (v. 46). These were the religious lawyers, those who drew up wills and so on for people, many of whom were semi-literate at best. In the English language, for example, how easy it is to add an 'n' to change 'one of you has won first prize' to '*n*one of you…' We don't need much imagination to see how easily the system could be worked for a lawyer's own pecuniary advantage, perhaps providing the wherewithal for those eye-catching flowing robes (v. 46). Such first-century religious hucksters have too many imitators in the 21st century. The occasional exposés by investigative journalists, highlighting the lavish lifestyles and financial impropriety of some of the putatively devout, bring great discredit on religion generally and the Christian faith particularly. Jesus' words 'punished most severely' (v. 47) are intended to shock any would-be get-rich-quick religious predator.

The connection to the second paragraph of today's reading is somewhat obscured by the chapter division, for the narrative flows naturally on to highlight one particular widow. The Archbishop of El Salvador Oscar Romero was an outspoken critic of the injustices he witnessed all around him in his society, especially those perpetrated by the powerful rich against the defenceless poor. Regularly threatened with death, he was assassinated while offering mass on 24 March 1980. Among his many penetrative observations, he is credited with saying, 'When I feed the poor, they call me a saint. When I ask why the poor are poor, they call me a communist.'[20] When we ask why this particular widow was so poor, it was probably because the religious hypocrites had taken advantage of her widowed state; like the fatherless and others who were disempowered, she was among the most vulnerable in society. Rightly, we should applaud and admire this woman's devotion, generosity and sacrifice. Certainly, the Lord did (vv. 3–4). It also suggests an encouragement for those who feel they have been exploited, financially and in other ways, by a church or some spiritual charlatan. Clearly, this lady was contributing money to a 'lost cause'. Nevertheless, her intention was to give to God, out of love and gratitude to him. Even when our gifts have been misappropriated, the Lord still notes our intentions. Jesus saw the widow and her gift, as he sees ours, a sobering thought indeed (v. 2).

Many years ago, a friend took an afternoon meeting in a church. At the back of the church was an offertory box, in which he placed a half-crown, in today's prices the equivalent of a gallon of petrol. At the end of the service, he was told that the church always gave the preacher whatever was in the offering. He duly received his half-crown back! Another friend quipped, 'You know, if you had put more in, you'd have got more out!' In the light of this passage, along with a prayerful meditation on 2 Corinthians 9:6–11, we might be encouraged to 'go and do likewise!'

Back to the future

Some of his disciples were remarking about how the temple was adorned with beautiful stones and with gifts dedicated to God. But Jesus said, 'As for what you see here, the time will come when not one stone will be left on another; every one of them will be thrown down.'

'Teacher,' they asked, 'when will these things happen? And what will be the sign that they are about to take place?'

He replied: 'Watch out that you are not deceived. For many will come in my name, claiming, "I am he," and, "The time is near". Do not follow them. When you hear of wars and uprisings, do not be frightened. These things must happen first, but the end will not come right away.'

'When you see Jerusalem being surrounded by armies, you will know that its desolation is near. Then let those who are in Judea flee to the mountains, let those in the city get out, and let those in the country not enter the city.'

'Be careful, or your hearts will be weighed down with carousing, drunkenness and the anxieties of life, and that day will close on you suddenly like a trap. For it will come on all those who live on the face of the whole earth. Be always on the watch, and pray that you may be able to escape all that is about to happen, and that you may be able to stand before the Son of Man.'

LUKE 21:5–9, 20–21, 34–36

When it comes to speculation, chapters like this are a happy hunting ground for every prophetic prognosticator. From earliest days, believers and unbelievers have sought ways and means to find out the shape of the future. Famously, for example, William Miller was confident that the end of the world would happen on 21 March 1843. Accordingly, he and a few friends climbed a hill and awaited the end. By the morning of 22 March, I suppose it dawned upon him that he might have been mistaken! So what is it we need to know in order that we are 'not deceived' (v. 8)?

One of the helpful tools in my library is a book entitled *Synopsis of the Four Gospels*, which compares the slightly different ways the four writers tell the story of Jesus, so that I don't have to keep four places open in my Bible at the same time. It's of particular benefit when reading this passage on the destruction of the temple and Jerusalem. Mark, for example, tells us who the four questioners were (Mark 13:3), while Matthew supplies a fuller form of the disciples' question: 'When will this happen, and what will be the sign of your coming and of the end of the age?' (Matthew 24:3). So there are two foci in the passage: the more imminent destruction of the temple and the fall of Jerusalem, and the less imminent return of Jesus. There are several imperatives we need to heed.

First, the need to *wise up*. Some people think Christians have two brains: one's lost and the other is out looking for it. In other words, they are naive. In contrast, Jesus tells us to 'watch out' for there is massive deception about, with false Christ's appearing (v. 8). When I was a minister in the East End of London, in the early 1980s, a certain Benjamin Crème informed the world that in Brick Lane, just down the road from my church, the Christ had returned. He challenged the press to come and find him. I didn't bother. Knowing and believing these words of Jesus should make us immediately sceptical of such claims.

Second, there is the need to *trust deeply*, for there will be tough days ahead with wars, natural disasters and cosmic signs (vv. 9–10, 25). In addition, direct physical persecution of believers would ensue, some from vested religious interests and some even from one's own family (vv. 12–19). When it does, even if it means 'death' for some, yet 'not a hair of your head will perish', as believers gain life by 'standing firm' (vv. 16, 18–19). Isn't that a contradiction? No, it is an outworking of our Lord's words not to fear those who can only 'kill the body and after that can do no more' (Luke 12:4: Matthew 10:28). Death does not separate us from the presence and love of God.

Third, there's the need to *look up*. When we look around there are such terrible things recorded in this passage and abounding in our world today, amply illustrated by our daily news. Like Nebuchadnezzar of old, we may feel we are losing our sanity. That bad man, however, passed on a great tip: 'I… raised my eyes towards heaven, and my sanity was restored' (Daniel 4:34). Many people pay exorbitant amounts for a facelift. Here's a free faithlift: the Lord Jesus is coming 'with power and great glory', so we are to 'lift up our heads' because the full package of redemption is about to arrive (vv. 27–28).

Fourth, God's people were to *get out*. In the ancient world, when a city was under siege, the path of wisdom was to stay within its walls. Here Jesus says the opposite. The result was that although over a million people perished as Jerusalem fell, many from starvation, Christians had fled in their droves to Pella. Why? Because they believed their Lord's words. That is biblical faith – acting on the words of Jesus that 'will never pass away' (v. 33).

Finally, they were to *speak up*. Increasingly today, the pressure is on Christians to be seen and not heard, and preferably not to be seen either in some quarters. Christian witness of course must be backed up by lifestyle, letting our light shine (Matthew 5:16). But at its heart it is also verbal: 'bear testimony to me… for I will give you words and wisdom' (vv. 13, 15).

How do we prepare for the end of the world? When John Wesley was asked how he would prepare if he knew Jesus was coming the next day, he apparently produced his diary, mentioned rising at 4.00 am for prayer, riding to Bedford to speak at 6.00 am at its jail, then 8.00 am in the town square and so on. In other words, it was business as usual whether or not his Lord returned that day. How do we prepare for the end of our personal world? 'Be always on the watch, and pray… that you may be able to stand before the Son of Man' (v. 36). And to kneel before him every day as if it is our last.

Wednesday

Red-letter day

They left and found things just as Jesus had told them. So, they prepared the Passover.

When the hour came, Jesus and his apostles reclined at the table. And he said to them, 'I have eagerly desired to eat this Passover with you before I suffer. For I tell you, I will not eat it again until it finds fulfilment in the kingdom of God.'

After taking the cup, he gave thanks and said, 'Take this and divide it among you. For I tell you I will not drink again from the fruit of the vine until the kingdom of God comes.'

And he took bread, gave thanks and broke it, and gave it to them, saying, 'This is my body given for you; do this in remembrance of me.'

In the same way, after the supper he took the cup, saying, 'This cup is the new covenant in my blood, which is poured out for you.'

LUKE 22:13–20

Louis Klopsch was an enterprising immigrant American journalist, a contemporary of the great evangelist D.L. Moody and eminent preacher Revd T. De Witt Talmage, his minister. On 19 June 1899, his eye fell upon Luke 22:20: 'This cup is the new covenant in my blood, which is poured out for you.' Seeing the possible symbolism of blood, and checking it with Dr Talmage, he concluded that it would be a great idea if the words of Christ were printed in red. Thus was born the familiar red-letter Bibles, where the words of Jesus are highlighted in a particular shade of brick red, according to one publisher.[21] It became an outstanding bestseller. Although some may quibble at his innovation, he had hit upon a rich vein of biblical theology, not only in the direct words attributed to Jesus but also the bloodline of scripture itself. But first, we turn to the setting of the words.

If Jerusalem was to be 'trampled on by the Gentiles' (Luke 21:24) and the temple, along with its priesthood, sacrifices and cultus, was to disappear within 40 years of our Lord's words, how and where were believers to worship? It's a question a Samaritan woman raised, whether Jerusalem or their mountain was the place of worship, to which Jesus replied that a time was coming when such concerns would be irrelevant. Rather, since God is Spirit, 'true worshippers will worship the Father in the Spirit and in truth' (John 4:23). How and where? Part of the answer is supplied by this Passover meal that the Lord 'eagerly desired' (v. 15) to eat with his disciples and that he invested with new significance and meaning. It also highlights the close relationship between the testaments of our Bibles.

In that ancient Passover event, God himself had intervened to rescue his people when they were in bondage. A mediator had been raised up to stand between them and God. And on that never-to-be-forgotten night, it was the blood of a lamb that protected them from destruction. The Lord then led them through a form of baptism in the Red Sea and via a wilderness experience, accompanied all the way by his Spirit, until they eventually reached the promised land. Does that sound familiar? It should, for it wonderfully mirrors the Christian pilgrim's story, as we travel to a promised land under the auspices of a 'new covenant' in Christ's 'blood' (v. 20). Indeed, these three words are vastly important for faith:

- *Blood* in scripture has strong, sacrificial overtones of a life violently taken, in this context for the benefit of others as a ransom: 'poured out for' us. Christ is indeed 'our Passover lamb' (1 Corinthians 5:7).
- *New* does not simply mean brand new, but something that has been renewed and becomes immeasurably better than it was before.

- *Covenant* is not merely an agreement or contract between equals. Rather, it is 'a relationship between God and man [*sic*], entered into on the sole initiative of the grace and love of God'.[22] It partakes of something of the nature of a 'Last Will and Testament', enacted when someone has died and in which they have expressed their wishes for the disbursement of their property. So, our Bibles are divided into old and new *covenants* or *testaments*, expressing God's choice for the disbursement of his riches. These two ideas – covenant and testament/will – are brought together in the book of Hebrews:

> For this reason Christ is the mediator of a new covenant, that those who are called may receive the promised eternal inheritance – now that he has died as a ransom to set them free from the sins committed under the first covenant. In the case of a will, it is necessary to prove the death of the one who made it, because a will is in force only when somebody has died; it never takes effect while the one who made it is living
>
> HEBREWS 9:15–17 (emphasis added)

I have highlighted 'covenant' and 'will' here because they are the same word in Greek, 'testament'. Applied to our Bibles, we might have called its two parts the old and new wills. Some time ago, a dearly loved friend remembered me in his will. As a result of his kindness and generosity, and through no merit or expectation on my part, I received a small legacy. As Jesus eats a Passover meal with his disciples, and invests the bread and wine shared with the massive significance of his cross, much, much more is coming our way than a small legacy: a 'promised eternal inheritance' (Hebrews 9:15). Wherever we are today, whatever our circumstances, in Christ we are beneficiaries of his boundless riches. It was said of Pip, an orphan with seemingly few prospects, that in fact he had, in the title of Dickens' great novel, *Great Expectations*. In Christ, so have we.

Maundy Thursday

Gethsemane

Jesus went out as usual to the Mount of Olives, and his disciples followed him. On reaching the place, he said to them, 'Pray that you will not fall into temptation.' He withdrew about a stone's throw beyond them, knelt down and prayed, 'Father, if you are willing, take this cup from me; yet not my will, but yours be done.' An angel from heaven appeared to him and strengthened him. And being in anguish, he prayed more earnestly, and his sweat was like drops of blood falling to the ground. When he rose from prayer and went back to the disciples, he found them asleep, exhausted from sorrow. 'Why are you sleeping?' he asked them. 'Get up and pray so that you will not fall into temptation.'

LUKE 22:39–46

I recall vividly my first visit to Israel, in 1990. It was at the height of the build-up to the first Gulf war. Tensions were mounting, the tourist trade had collapsed and the threat of Scud missiles landing in Israel was soon to be realised. Yet here I was leading a party of over 30 other pilgrims on a visit to the garden of Gethsemane, which felt like an oasis of tranquillity amid the shifting sands of violence. At least one of the olive trees in the garden apparently dated back to the time of our Lord. The tree was there *that* night, silently witnessing the scene of today's meditation. We can't be there literally, but we are invited to overhear this immense drama as the Son of God battles the encircling forces of despair, darkness and ensuing death.

Luke, a doctor, underlines the sheer horror of this scene. He records the Lord's sweat appeared 'like drops of blood falling to the ground', literally a 'thrombosis of blood'. This is not so much an anatomical phenomenon, since it is '*like* drops of blood'. Rather, it emphasises the emotional intensity of what Jesus was suffering, *agonia* being the Greek word, from which 'agony' is derived (v. 44). And such agony is recorded after angelic strengthening (v. 43). The cause of it is 'the cup' of suffering which he will soon drink in all its bitterness on the cross (v. 42). But why such distress? Luke later informs us that 'darkness came over the whole land until three in the afternoon, for the sun stopped shining' (23:44–45). But it is both Matthew and Mark who record what is termed 'The Cry of Dereliction': 'My God, my God, why have you forsaken me?' (Matthew 27:46; Mark 15:34). This cry prompted the German theologian Jürgen Moltmann to write of the Father and Son, inseparable and eternally one by the Spirit, experiencing a rupture in their relationship on the cross. He draws attention to the phenomenon of the 'the Fatherlessness of the Son' being 'matched by the Sonlessness of the Father', however brief that experience may have been.[23] Certainly, 'we may not know, we cannot tell what pains he had to bear',[24] for the Lord's cross is not only something experienced extrinsically by God 'up in heaven' but, in ways unimaginable to us, as something intrinsic to the very life of God himself. For Jesus, as the Son of God, this is surely the source, in prospect, of his extreme suffering.

Of course, Gethsemane opens up many other avenues of thought. For example, some in the early church tried to suggest that Jesus only *appeared* to be a man. Here, there is stark reminder of his very real humanity: he's not less than human, flesh and blood, though far, far more. Again, some people confuse temptation with sin. But, as somebody put it, temptation is like the devil knocking at our door; it is only sin when we let him in. Ultimately, of course, the events in the garden, like the cross, resurrection and ascension of Jesus, are unique. At another level, Gethsemane is also, like the cross, resurrection and ascension, a paradigm for believers. As one hard-pressed friend put it to me, while going through an immense emotional crisis, 'Steve, there were no words in the dictionary of my soul to express my pain.' Whatever we have suffered, are facing and may yet encounter, in Jesus we have 'one who has been tempted in every way, just as we are – yet he did not sin'. So we discover that 'he is able to help those who are being tempted' (Hebrews 4:15, 2:18). The words of one of Frederick Faber's hymns are so appropriate when we feel we should chuck in the towel, go with the flow and capitulate to temptation:

Ever when tempted, make me see,
Beneath the olives' moon-pierced shade,
My God, alone, outstretched, and bruised,
And bleeding, on the earth He made;

And make me feel it was my sin,
As though no other sins there were,
That was to Him who bears the world
A load that He could scarcely bear.

Frederick Faber (1814–53)

Can I make it through my Gethsemane? 'He will also keep you firm to the end, so that you will be blameless on the day of our Lord Jesus Christ. God is faithful, who has called you into fellowship with his Son, Jesus Christ our Lord' (1 Corinthians 1:8–9). Jesus trusted his Father. So should we.

Good Friday

....

A dying thief, a living hope

There was a written notice above him, which read: THIS IS THE KING OF THE JEWS.

One of the criminals who hung there hurled insults at him: 'Aren't you the Messiah? Save yourself and us!'

But the other criminal rebuked him. 'Don't you fear God,' he said, 'since you are under the same sentence? We are punished justly, for we are getting what our deeds deserve. But this man has done nothing wrong.'

Then he said, 'Jesus, remember me when you come into your kingdom.'

Jesus answered him, 'Truly I tell you, today you will be with me in paradise.'

LUKE 23:38–43

'These verses… deserve to be printed in letters of gold. They have probably been the salvation of myriads of souls,' commented the great J.C. Ryle, the first Anglican bishop of my hometown of Liverpool.[25] But not everyone, for here are three men: one died *in* sin; another *to* sin; the third *for* sin.

It is often assumed when people are in deep straits, especially approaching the end of life, that a 'just in case there is a God' insurance-policy faith kicks in. But pain, suffering and certain death do not necessarily lead to a death-bed conversion, as the first criminal's behaviour highlights. Like the rulers who 'sneered' (v. 35) and the soldiers who 'mocked' (v. 36), this man 'hurled insults' at Jesus (v. 39). Terrifyingly, he illustrates that it is possible to be near to Jesus, speak to Jesus and die with Jesus, and yet be lost. Someone wisely remarked that the essence of heaven is to say to God, 'Your will be done', while the essence of hell is when God says to us, 'Your will be done!' This man was a successful rebel to the end.

In stark contrast, there hangs another thief. Both Matthew and Mark record that both criminals 'heaped insults' on Jesus (Matthew 27:44; Mark 15:32). So what changed his attitude to Christ? Commentators have speculated that he had heard Jesus preach. Others, that he knew that both Pilate and Herod thought Jesus innocent. Yet others, that his conscience was pricked by our Lord's prayer for his enemies and his calm demeanour in death. Who knows? What is clear, however, is that he feared God, owning up to his wrongdoing (vv. 40–41). He believed, despite the evidence to the contrary, that Jesus did have a kingdom (as the title on Jesus' cross inadvertently advertised), and he wanted to be part of it (vv. 38, 42). He had no good works to offer, no possibility of enjoying the sacraments, no church to join. But he repented, believed and was saved. Amazing grace!

And why is Jesus there, between two criminals (v. 33)? A thief too? He fed the 5,000. A murderer? He healed the sick and raised the dead. The victim of a miscarriage of justice? Undoubtedly, but he said he could call on 'twelve legions of angels' to deliver him (Matthew 26:53). So why is he there? Two charges emerge from the gospel records: blasphemy (Mark 14:64) and rebellion (Luke 23:14). The irony here is that the centurion confesses that Jesus is both 'a righteous man' and 'the Son of God' (Luke 23:47; Mark 15:39).

Truly, he had 'done nothing to deserve death' (Luke 23:15). We have! Don't we all stand as rebels before a holy God? Aren't there times when we feel the lure of almightiness, the blasphemy that we are kings of the castle, godlike creatures on earth without a God up there to whom we are accountable? The gospel comes to tell us of one who has taken the hit for our pride and folly. If the released felon Barabbas, 'thrown into prison for insurrection and murder' (23:25), had turned up at the cross, he might accurately have said,

'That man is there in my place, paying my price, dying my death, so I can go free!' But only Barabbas? Truly, 'We all, like sheep, have gone astray… and the Lord has laid on him the iniquity of us all'; for 'the Son of Man… [came] to serve, and to give his life as a ransom for many' (Isaiah 53:6; Mark 10:45).

A church I visited years ago had a sermon in stone on an outside wall. It consisted of three crosses, the one on the left pointing inwards towards the central cross and the one on the right pointing away. Wisely, Bishop Ryle reminds us: 'One thief was saved that no sinner might despair; but only one, that no sinner might presume.'[26] Which way am I looking as the Lord of glory gives his life as a ransom for the world?

Holy Saturday

Dead and gone?

It was now about noon, and darkness came over the whole land until three in the afternoon, for the sun stopped shining. And the curtain of the temple was torn in two. Jesus called out with a loud voice, 'Father, into your hands I commit my spirit.' When he had said this, he breathed his last.

Now there was a man named Joseph, a member of the Council, a good and upright man, who had not consented to their decision and action. He came from the Judean town of Arimathea, and he himself was waiting for the kingdom of God. Going to Pilate, he asked for Jesus' body. Then he took it down, wrapped it in linen cloth and placed it in a tomb cut in the rock, one in which no one had yet been laid.

LUKE 23:44–46, 50–53

For as long as I can remember, I have been intrigued by life's unavoidable question, 'What happens when we die?' Some decades ago, while I was involved in doctoral research about our individual post-mortem state, many theologians seemed to be reluctant to think about the subject, designating it a *terra incognita*, an unknown, uncharted region. Is that all that can be said, a resort to a reverent agnosticism?

On the other side of the coin, every week millions of Christians confess, in the words of the Apostles' Creed, that Jesus 'was crucified, died, and was buried. He descended *into hell.*' Did he? A few ambiguous passages suggest he might have (e.g. Ephesians 4:9; 1 Peter 3:19–20; 4:6). Conversely, there stands our Lord's words to the dying thief, 'today you will be with me in paradise' (Luke 23:43). What can be said about our Lord's post-mortem experience, after he prayed 'Father, into your hands I commit my spirit' and 'breathed his last' (v. 46)?

Some have speculated that our Lord descended to hell to suffer further, experiencing solidarity with departed sinful human beings. But this essentially calls into question the finished work of the cross. For Luke reminds us that 'the curtain of the temple was torn in two' (v. 45), indicating, as other scriptures will expand on, that the way into God's presence has now been opened (e.g. Hebrews 10:19–22). In the suffering he bore on the cross, contemplated in Gethsemane as we noted in a previous meditation, Jesus experienced the 'terrible torments of a condemned and forsaken man'[27] in our place.

On the other hand, a majority report of theologians down the centuries is summed up in the phrase 'the harrowing of hell'. Between his death and resurrection, the Lord marched into hell, as it were, and proclaimed his victory over death, the devil and all his dark powers. In other words, it is a victory procession, a lap of honour. But once again, I think, we miscue if we underestimate the reverberations directly from the finished work on the cross. It was there he 'cancelled the charge of our legal indebtedness… nailing it to the cross. And having disarmed the powers and authorities, he made a public spectacle of them, triumphing over them by the cross' (Colossians 2:14–15). As John's Gospel reminds us, the cry from the cross is 'It is finished' – accomplished, completed, fulfilled, consummated, paid, realised (John 19:30). If that is so, then in a real sense Christ has visited hell, in that his victory reverberates across the whole cosmos and beyond.

Is that victory still being proclaimed? In a remarkable passage, the apostle Paul tells us God's 'intent was that now, *through the church*, the manifold wisdom of God should be made known to the rulers and authorities in the heavenly realms' (Ephesians 3:10, emphasis added). In ways scarcely imaginable, individually and corporately,

Christians are living letters being written by the risen Christ and on display before invisible spectators. What an audience we have!

Before we leave our mediations on Holy Saturday, we pause to note the brave and loving act of Joseph of Arimathea, as he buried Jesus (vv. 52–53). Without realising it, he fulfilled Isaiah's ancient prophecy about Messiah's suffering: 'He was assigned a grave with the wicked' – indeed, for he was hung between two criminals as Luke noted (23:33) – 'and with the rich in his death' (Isaiah 53:9). Joseph was a 'rich man' (Matthew 27:57). Whatever our financial situation, we tend to be far more likely to see our personal expenses and comforts as essential, and our gifts accordingly measured and small. Not so with Joseph. He gave up a new, probably massively expensive, rock-hewn tomb.

A humorous story has done the rounds about his generosity: on his return home that evening, there was a reception party waiting for him, composed of his wife and family. They are appalled that he had not only given away the family tomb but also probably desecrated it for good, having placed a convicted criminal there. After all, 'Cursed is everyone who hangs on a tree' (Deuteronomy 21:23; Galatians 3:13). Joseph's reply? 'Don't worry. He's only borrowing it for the weekend!' Funny but true! To adopt and adapt the well-known sermon title: 'It's Saturday... but Sunday's coming!'

Easter Day

....

The short walk to freedom

Now that same day two of them were going to a village called Emmaus, about seven miles from Jerusalem. They were talking with each other about everything that had happened. As they talked and discussed these things with each other, Jesus himself came up and walked along with them; but they were kept from recognising him.

He asked them, 'What are you discussing together as you walk along?'

They stood still, their faces downcast. One of them, named Cleopas, asked him, 'Are you the only one visiting Jerusalem who does not know the things that have happened there in these days?'

'What things?' he asked.

'About Jesus of Nazareth,' they replied. 'He was a prophet, powerful in word and deed before God and all the people. The chief priests and our rulers handed him over to be sentenced to death, and they crucified him; but we had hoped that he was the one who was going to redeem Israel. And what is more, it is the third day since all this took place. In addition, some of our women amazed us. They went to the tomb early this morning but didn't find his body. They came and told us that they had seen a vision of angels, who said he was alive. Then some of our companions went to the tomb and found it just as the women had said, but they did not see Jesus.'

He said to them, 'How foolish you are, and how slow to believe all that the prophets have spoken! Did not the Messiah have to suffer these things and then enter his glory?' And beginning with Moses and all the Prophets, he explained to them what was said in all the Scriptures concerning himself.

As they approached the village to which they were going, Jesus continued on as if he were going further. But they urged him strongly, 'Stay with us, for it is nearly evening; the day is almost over.' So he went in to stay with them.

When he was at the table with them, he took bread, gave thanks, broke it and began to give it to them. Then their eyes were opened and they recognised him, and he disappeared from their sight. They asked each other, 'Were not our hearts burning within us while he talked with us on the road and opened the Scriptures to us?'

They got up and returned at once to Jerusalem. There they found the Eleven and those with them, assembled together and saying, 'It is true! The Lord has risen and has appeared to Simon.' Then the two told what had happened on the way, and how Jesus was recognised by them when he broke the bread.

LUKE 24:13–35

I had the privilege, although it took me years afterwards to realise it, of attending a traditional boys' grammar school, with its heavy emphasis on the classics, Greek and Latin. I suspect it had something to do with the head teacher, an Oxbridge classics scholar, who occasionally led the morning religious assembly. My recollection is that whenever he did, he invariably read this familiar story, perhaps because he was a practising Quaker and wanted to emphasise the 'burning heart' experience (v. 32) of these two initially dejected characters. As we follow this narrative, we discover other parts of our bodies that also need to be engaged.

Downcast faces (v. 17)

Imagine some of the headlines that could be run today: Easter Sunday! Christ is Risen! Sin Atoned For! Death Vanquished! Satan

Defeated! But these two are miserable, clearly disappointed with Jesus, whom they hoped would 'redeem Israel' (v. 21), and totally bewildered by an empty tomb (vv. 22–24). Does today find you likewise disappointed and bewildered? Christ may be risen but so far, for all the difference it makes for you, he might as well be dead.

Ready tongues (vv. 14–24)

For some of us, our problem is we talk too much. But these two are legitimately engaged in what we might quaintly call 'holy conversation' (vv. 14–15). Clearly, they had a good grasp of the gospel's basic facts: Jesus' life and ministry, suffering and death, and the empty tomb. On Easter morning, it's vital to believe such facts, for there is no risen Christ without an empty tomb. But like the soldiers who guarded Jesus, we may find an empty tomb and not the risen Lord (Matthew 28:4).

Listening ears (vv.25–27)

Bradycardia is a condition where the heart beats very slowly. This is the word here, 'slow of heart'; but it is everything to do with their spiritual not physical hearts. How do we get to know the living Christ? We note our Lord's method was to take them to their Bibles. When the Psalms (v. 44) are added to 'Moses and all the Prophets' (v. 27), as here, we have the 39 books we refer to as the Old Testament. What a Bible study that was! One of the courses integral to our training at Moorlands has the daunting title 'Hermeneutics'. In Greek, it is related to the word which is here translated 'explained' (v. 27), or 'interpreted' in other translations. According to Jesus, it is 'the Scriptures that testify about' him (John 5:39). In other words, he is the key to properly understanding the first part of the Bible, whether such appears in prophecy, type, parallel, paradigm, etc. But we also need divine assistance, asking the Lord who 'opened their minds so they could understand the Scriptures' (v. 45) to open ours too. As a youth, I used to sing a simple chorus: 'Read your Bible, pray every day, *if you want to grow*.' Indeed! But I'd like to change the final phrase slightly, to 'if you want to *know*'. The purpose of our Bibles, the word of the Lord, is that we might know, and know better, the Lord of the word.

Opened eyes and burning hearts (vv. 28–32)

In many parts of the world hospitality is a sacred duty, and these two were insistent that Jesus should accept their offer. We are not told what opened their eyes (v. 31), when previously 'their eyes were kept from recognising him' (v. 16, RSV). Some have suggested that, as Jesus broke the bread, they saw the nail prints in his hands (vv. 30, 35, 40). Perhaps, but divine action lay behind the revelatory moment, as it always does. The objective facts of an empty tomb and a risen Lord were now matched by a subjective experience of their 'hearts burning within' (v. 32). That sort of thing happens when 'Jesus himself', initially unrecognisable, draws near to us (v. 15) and we pray, 'Stay with us' (v. 29). Perhaps we missed him in the morning of life or in the noonday of our busyness, and the shadows gather, 'it's nearly evening', and our 'day is almost over'. May we today invite him to 'stay with us', and find that he has done so (v. 29).

Willing feet (vv. 33–35)

Excellent Bible study, burning hearts and deep spiritual experiences are not an end in themselves. Quickly, these two want to share it with others (vv. 33–35), and those others in turn with the whole world, 'as witnesses of these things' (v. 48). Happy Easter!

Epilogue

Our man in heaven

In my former book, Theophilus, I wrote about all that Jesus began to do and to teach until the day he was taken up to heaven, after giving instructions through the Holy Spirit to the apostles he had chosen. After his suffering, he presented himself to them and gave many convincing proofs that he was alive. He appeared to them over a period of forty days and spoke about the kingdom of God. On one occasion, while he was eating with them, he gave them this command: 'Do not leave Jerusalem, but wait for the gift my Father promised, which you have heard me speak about. For John baptised with water, but in a few days you will be baptised with the Holy Spirit.'

Then they gathered around him and asked him, 'Lord, are you at this time going to restore the kingdom to Israel?'

He said to them: 'It is not for you to know the times or dates the Father has set by his own authority. But you will receive power when the Holy Spirit comes on you; and you will be my witnesses in Jerusalem, and in all Judea and Samaria, and to the ends of the earth.'

After he said this, he was taken up before their very eyes, and a cloud hid him from their sight.

They were looking intently up into the sky as he was going, when suddenly two men dressed in white stood beside them. 'Men of Galilee,' they said, 'why do you stand here looking into the sky? This same Jesus, who has been taken from you into heaven, will come back in the same way you have seen him go into heaven.'

ACTS 1:1–11

As we come to our final meditation today, 'Do not leave Jerusalem' (v. 4) is not the Lord's final word, as if the disciples are to stay indefinitely there. Soon, very soon, will be the time to leave and impact the nations for Christ as his witnesses (v. 8). For that, however, they are going to need far more than mere money, methods, media and good management, like too many churches and organisations today are tempted to rely on. How is the church to make it through to the Lord's return (v. 11)? And, at a personal level, how are we to make it through until we enter 'the Jerusalem that is above', 'the city with foundations, whose architect and builder is God' (Galatians 4:26; Hebrews 11:10)?

Disciples who are certain of their Lord's resurrection

Those in the upper room (v. 13) had no doubts about Christ's death. There were so many who had been eyewitnesses of it. But there was also an 'after' to 'his suffering' – 'many convincing proofs that he was alive' (v. 3). His aliveness is no mere temporary resurrection, like those the Lord raised in his ministry, such as Lazarus. Nor is it some ghostly appearance: 'a ghost does not have flesh and bones, as you see I have', as the Lord strongly asserted (Luke 24:39). Some have quibbled at the empty-tomb narratives, the more sophisticated talking about some sort of 'spiritual' resurrection without any physicality. Such would have seemed absurd to first-century, Jewish believers. The beautiful Garden Tomb in Jerusalem, which represents what Christ's burial place might have been like, has some words from Matthew etched into the oak door: 'HE IS NOT HERE – FOR HE IS RISEN' (see Matthew 28:6). We might appropriately call the tomb of Jesus a cenotaph, which literally means 'empty grave'. Yet, somehow, he is still the 'same Jesus' (v. 11). His death and resurrection were to open the way for the gift the Father had promised (v. 4), namely 'God's empowering presence',[28] as one writer calls the Holy Spirit, the baptiser and energiser of the church for its worldwide mission (vv. 5, 8).

Believers who are convinced of Christ's reign

It should be no surprise that the Lord's ascension has been dismissed as some form of pre-scientific, flat-earth, three-decker cosmology. Yet the text insists that what happened was 'before their very eyes', that it involved 'sight', a 'looking intently up', a 'looking into the sky', and that the disciples had 'seen him go into heaven' (vv. 9–11). With typical clarity, C.S. Lewis asserts, 'If the spectators say they saw first a short vertical movement and then a vague luminosity… and then nothing – have we any reason to object?'[29]

The rest of the New Testament will fill out the implications and meaning of the ascension in various ways. For example, it means Jesus is enthroned as 'Prince', the 'Lord of all', who is 'far above all rule and authority', with 'angels, authorities and powers in submission to him' (Acts 5:31; 10:36; Ephesians 1:21; 1 Peter 3:22). There is never an 'energy crisis', when we have the inexhaustible Christ! Moreover, he is a high priest, one who lifts up hands to bless and ever lives to intercede for his people (Luke 24:50; Romans 8:34; Hebrews 7:25). There is one at God's right hand who fully understands and ever stands with us. How? Because he is the provider, having 'received from the Father the promised Holy Spirit', he pours out his gift and graces on his people (Acts 2:33). Finally, he is also our pioneer, the trailblazer (Hebrews 2:10; 12:2), the one who has gone before us to 'prepare a place' for us (John 14:2). How majestic is Jesus – prince, priest, provider, pioneer.

Christians who are confident of Christ's return

How many times do we hear or perhaps have ourselves said, 'I don't know what the world is coming to!' We ought to: 'This same Jesus... will come back' (v. 11). For many years, the UK had a mobile network operator called Orange UK. Its catchy slogan was 'The future's bright – the future's Orange'. It wasn't: it merged with another company and has disappeared as a brand. But since Jesus is risen, reigning and intending to return, 'The future's bright – the future's Christ.' Onwards and upwards, then, to God's everlasting city and eternal kingdom. Hope to see you there!

Notes

1   Amy Carmichael, *Towards Jerusalem* (SPCK, 1967).
2   John Lennox, *Seven Days that Divide the World* (Zondervan, 2011), p. 11.
3   Alasdair Paine, *The First Chapters of Everything: How Genesis 1—4 explains our world* (Christian Focus, 2014).
4   Steve Brady, *The Incredible Journey: Christmas from Genesis to Jesus* (BRF, 2011).
5   E.A. Speiser, 'The rivers of paradise', in R.S. Hess and D.T. Tsumura (eds), *I Studied Inscriptions from Before the Flood* (Eisenbrauns, 1994), p. 175, n. 18. (I am indebted to Alistair McKitterick, one of my colleagues, for this helpful quote.)
6   C.S. Lewis, 'The weight of glory', in *C.S. Lewis Essay Collection and Other Short Pieces* (HarperCollins, 2000), pp. 98–9.
7   From 'Invictus' (1875) by William Ernest Henley (1849–1903).
8   Quoted by A.F. Kirkpatrick, *The Book of Psalms* (Cambridge, 1902), p. vi.
9   Derek Kidner, *Psalms 73–150* (IVP, 1975), p. 431.
10 W.S. Plumer, *Psalms* (Banner of Truth, 1975), p. 1124.
11 'NHS spends £780,000 a day on antidepressants', *Pharma Times online*, 15 July 2016.
12 After Dale Carnegie's bestselling self-help book, *How to Win Friends and Influence People* (1936).
13 Josephus, *Antiquities* 11.5.8.
14 Douglas Murray, *The Spectator*, 6 February 2017.
15 Dietrich Bonhoeffer, *The Cost of Discipleship* (SCM, 1959), p. 79.
16 See Eberhard Bethge, *Dietrich Bonhoeffer* (Collins, 1970), p. 788. The English translation uses the word 'streets' for the German original's 'Boulevard'. I have paraphrased Bethge's 'arcane discipline' and 'worldliness' to 'spirituality' and 'worldly involvement', respectively.
17 Rabbie Burns, 'To a louse on seeing one on a lady's bonnet, at church', 1786.
18 C.S. Lewis, *The Screwtape Letters* (Geoffrey Bles, 1942), Letter XXVI.
19 Helmut Thielicke, *The Waiting Father* (James Clark, 1960).

20 In fact, it appears that it was another Catholic Archbishop, from Brazil, Hélder Pessoa Câmara (1909–99), who first said it. See https://en.wikipedia.org/wiki/Hélder_Câmara, accessed 17 May 2017.

21 Steve Eng, 'The story behind: red letter Bible editions', *Bible Collectors' World*, January–March 1986.

22 William Barclay, *The Making of the Bible* (Saint Andrew Press, 1979), p. 49.

23 Jürgen Moltmann, *The Crucified God* (SCM, 1974), p. 243.

24 From 'There is a Green Hill Far Away', Cecil Frances Alexander (1818–74).

25 J.C. Ryle, *Expository Thoughts on the Gospels: St. Luke, Vol. 2* (James Clarke, 1969), pp. 469ff.

26 Ryle, *Expository Thoughts on the Gospels*, pp. 471–2.

27 There is a brief article by Dr Justin Stratis, 'Did Jesus descend into hell?', available on the website of Trinity College, Bristol, where he is a tutor in Christian doctrine, and for which I acknowledge my debt of gratitude in preparing this chapter. See www.trinitycollegebristol.ac.uk/blog/kingdom-learning/did-jesus-descend-into-hell.

28 Gordon D. Fee, *God's Empowering Presence* (Hendrickson, 1994).

29 C.S. Lewis, *Miracles* (Fontana, 1960), p. 160.

Explore the freeing, life-changing nature of forgiveness...

As we move from Ash Wednesday to Easter Day, daily reflections and prayers help us to experience the living power of the cross of Christ through biblical and modern-day stories of wrongdoing and forgiveness. Our journey through Lent will deepen our response to God's love and, as we allow the Holy Spirit to do his work, we will see spiritual transformation in our lives today.

The Living Cross
Exploring God's gift of forgiveness and new life
Amy Boucher Pye
978 0 85746 512 2 £8.99

brfonline.org.uk

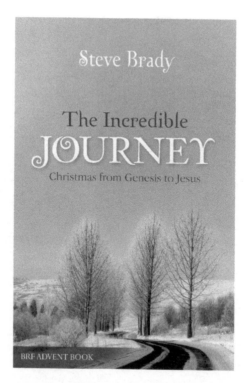

The Bible presents the ultimate adventure – God's incredible, personal journey to the human race, which he loves with an amazing love, despite its repeated rejection of him. The story culminates in the coming of Jesus Christ, the incarnate God, in the events we celebrate every Christmas. This book of readings for Advent and Christmas shows how Jesus has come to take us home to God, no matter what our starting point.

The Incredible Journey
Christmas from Genesis to Jesus
Steve Brady
978 0 85746 003 5 £7.99

brfonline.org.uk

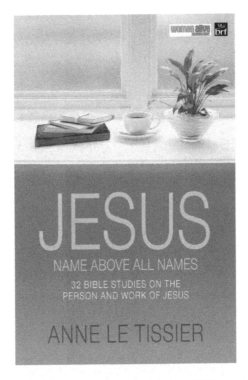

This book offers straightforward, devotionally based Bible study material on 32 names and titles ascribed to Jesus in scripture. From 'Advocate' to 'Word of God', the studies consider what we can learn about who Jesus is and what he has done for us from these different names and titles. The material includes extended reflection on the theme, questions for response, prayers and suggestions for further Bible reading. Prepared from articles originally published in *Woman Alive* magazine, this book is ideal for small group use or individual Quiet Day or retreat reading.

Jesus: Name Above All Names
32 Bible studies on the person and work of Jesus
Anne Le Tissier
978 0 85746 085 1   £8.99

brfonline.org.uk

Transforming
lives and communities

Christian growth and understanding of the Bible

Resourcing individuals, groups and leaders in churches for their own spiritual journey and for their ministry

Church outreach in the local community

Offering three programmes that churches are embracing to great effect as they seek to engage with their local communities and transform lives

Teaching Christianity in primary schools

Working with children and teachers to explore Christianity creatively and confidently

Children's and family ministry

Working with churches and families to explore Christianity creatively and bring the Bible alive

Visit **brf.org.uk** for more information on BRF's work
Review this book on Twitter using **#BRFconnect**

brf.org.uk

The Bible Reading Fellowship (BRF) is a Registered Charity (No. 233280)